# From Compliance to Community

## ALFIE KOHN

Merrill
Prentice Hall

Upper Saddle River, New Jersey
Columbus, Ohio

**Library of Congress Cataloging-in-Publication Data**
Kohn, Alfie.
    Beyond discipline : from compliance to community / Alfie Kohn.
      p.  cm.
    Originally published : Alexandria, Va. : ASCD, c1996.
    Includes bibliographical references (p.) and index.
    ISBN 0-13-093050-4
    1. School discipline—United States.   2. Classroom management—
United States  I. Title.
  LB3011.K64   2001
  371.5—dc21                                         00-068108

This special edition published by Merrill Education/Prentice Hall, Inc. by arrangement with the Association for Supervision and Curriculum Development.

**Vice President and Publisher:** Jeffery W. Johnston
**Executive Editor:** Kevin M. Davis
**Director of Marketing:** Kevin Flanagan
**Marketing Manager:** Amy June
**Marketing Coordinator:** Barbara Koontz

Designed by Karen Monaco.

This book was printed and bound by R. R. Donnelley & Sons Company. The cover was printed by The Lehigh Press, Inc.

The author is grateful for permission to use excerpts from the following sources:

*Becoming Responsible Learners: Strategies for Positive Classroom Management* by Mark Collis and Joan Dalton (Portsmouth, N.H.: Heinemann, 1990). Reprinted with the permission of Heinemann, a division of Reed Elsevier, Inc.

"Move On" from *Sunday in the Park with George*—Music & lyrics by Stephen Sondheim. Copyright 1984 by Rilting Music, Inc. All rights reserved. Used by permission.

10 9 8 7 6 5 4 3 2 1
ISBN: 0-13-093050-4

*For my daughter Abigail*

*The chief source of the "problem of discipline" in schools is that . . . a premium is put on physical quietude; on silence, on rigid uniformity of posture and movement; upon a machine-like simulation of the attitudes of intelligent interest. The teachers' business is to hold the pupils up to these requirements and to punish the inevitable deviations which occur.*

—John Dewey
*Democracy and Education*

# Beyond Discipline:
# From Compliance to Community

# FOREWORD

*Beyond Discipline: From Compliance to Community* is a refreshing look at the need to work with students to make decisions and solve problems—in essence, to create classrooms that are respectful of both adults and children. Alfie Kohn challenges our traditional thinking by suggesting that our first question about children should not be "How can we make them do what we want?" but rather "What do they require in order to flourish, and how can we provide those things?" Instead of trying to control students' behavior by, say, posting lists of consequences for misbehavior on the board, the teacher should focus on nourishing students' natural curiosity, helping them develop their problem-solving abilities and experience a sense of community.

Kohn criticizes many of the programs that offer what amount to recipes for taking care of discipline problems and maintaining controlled environments. He contends that many, if not all, of these packaged discipline programs focus on "handling" or "training" children, offering ways to outsmart them and methods for establishing consequences that ensure mindless compliance and control. Does such an environment, he asks, really promote meaningful learning?

Kohn's alternative is to make the classroom a community where students feel valued and respected, where care and trust have taken the place of restrictions and threats. In this environment, students have a major role in making meaningful decisions about their schooling and in designing educational communities in which they feel connected to one another and to adults.

The dissolution of punishments and rewards altogether is necessary in a community based on worth and caring. When punishments are used the teacher becomes an enforcer rather than the coach and nurturer; when rewards are used the teacher becomes the manipulator of mindless obedience.

Kohn artfully correlates how students act in school with what they are being asked to learn, describing clearly how unwelcome classroom behaviors can be directly traced to what children are asked to learn. The curriculum is part of the larger classroom context from which a student's behavior or misbehavior emerges. Kohn says that if we really want to make sense of how students act, then the curriculum must be scrutinized. Is it too simple, boring, without value, or lacking opportunities to interact with others? To get beyond discipline, we must expose children to a rich curriculum that extends their thinking, elicits their curiosity, and helps them reflect more skillfully on questions that are important to them.

In *Beyond Discipline,* Alfie Kohn offers readers a thoughtful guide for creating classrooms based on respect and dignity. To some, his approach may be unsettling because it differs, delightfully so, from traditional classroom management models in which teachers control students by promising them rewards or threatening them with punishment. But for the unencumbered seeker, moving beyond discipline can lead to a new understanding of the educational process. By relinquishing power and reconsidering the way we define and think about students' behavior, we can see the role of teachers with new clarity and, with our students, reconnect with the ideals of democracy.

—FRANCES FAIRCLOTH JONES
*ASCD President 1996–97*

# INTRODUCTION

A few years ago, I decided to start observing extraordinary classrooms. Whenever I was traveling and found myself with some extra time, I tracked down teachers in that area who were rumored to be doing interesting things and asked if I could visit them at work. I was particularly keen to see how they dealt with discipline problems. My assumption was that I could learn more from seeing how talented practitioners responded to obnoxious behavior than I could from reading books on the subject.

As it turned out, I rarely got the chance to see these teachers work their magic with misbehaving children because it seemed as though the children in their classes almost never misbehaved. Evidently I just happened to show up on unusually harmonious days— or else I wasn't staying long enough. After a while, however, it dawned on me that this pattern couldn't be explained just by my timing. These classrooms were characterized by a chronic absence of problems.

Even in schools where students are sent to the office to be disciplined, principals know that some teachers almost never need to do this. But why? Obviously there is something to the luck of the draw: the feel of a class, the characteristics of a given group of students and the way they interact, will vary from year to year. But how likely is it that certain teachers just happen to get dream classes every September?

Clearly, we need to look at the teachers themselves, not just at the kids who are assigned to them. These teachers seem to be doing something that makes it less likely that their students would want to, or need to, act in disturbing ways. During my visits, I've been struck not only by what such teachers are doing, and how successful it is, but by what they are *not* doing.

They are not concentrating on being effective disciplinarians.

This is partly because they have better things to do, and those better things are preventing problems from developing in the first place. But it's also because discipline—at least as that word is typically used—*actively interferes with what they are trying to accomplish*. It took me a while to figure that out and to be able to explain why I believe it's true. That's what I attempt to do in this book, and the result is likely to be not merely controversial but deeply unsettling to many readers. What other books have been doing to the old Listen-to-me-lecture, Memorize-these-facts, Fill-in-the-blanks, Keep-your-eyes-on-your-own-paper style of academic learning, this book tries to do to the field of classroom management. (Ironically, a lot of people who offer well-reasoned critiques of traditional academic learning take for granted a bundle of premises about the nonacademic side of what goes on in schools.)

The raison d'être of discipline or classroom management* is almost always to secure children's compliance with adults' demands. Thus, it is assumed, teachers have a responsibility to get and maintain control of their classrooms. In doing so, they are encouraged to focus on students' behaviors and attempt to alter those that they, for whatever reason, deem inappropriate. Behavioral changes, in turn, are usually achieved by resorting to one or another extrinsic inducement, which is to say, some sort of reward or punishment.

It is in most respects a teacher-directed model, one in which expectations, rules, and consequences are imposed on students. And it is typically driven by a remarkably negative set of beliefs about the

---

* For reasons of convenience, I will be using these terms more or less interchangeably. Some writers understandably prefer to define *discipline* as a subset of classroom management that deals only with responses to misbehavior. Others, meanwhile, including some who may be sympathetic to my critique, are anxious to rehabilitate the word *discipline* and therefore take pains to distinguish it from punishment. I want to be clear from the beginning about my use of these words so that we can separate semantic from substantive disagreements. My reason for writing this book is not to quibble about certain language but to challenge deeply held assumptions and widely accepted practices.

nature of children. But whenever things go wrong in such class-rooms—which is often—the approach itself is rarely blamed. It is the children who are said to be incorrigible, or the teachers who are faulted for being insufficiently firm or skillful. "Just look at our schools!" the educational commentators cry. "What we need is . . ." more of the same. Thus, the more we discipline, the more need there is to do so. The more classroom management programs disappoint, the more they create their own demand.

Be assured that the book you are holding does not offer yet an-other discipline plan to be placed alongside those that are already out there. I don't think we need another one—not when we already have Assertive Discipline and Cooperative Discipline, 21st Century Discipline and several programs called Positive Discipline, as well as Discipline with Dignity, Discipline with Love and Logic, and pro-grams where the discipline is described variously as collaborative, commonsense, creative, effective, gentle, innovative, judicious, and stress-free (in alphabetical order).

Some of these programs are remarkably autocratic, urging teach-ers to lay down the law with children and coerce them into compli-ance. The best that can be said about such advice is that it is straightforward: you know what you're getting. This is not always the case with what I will call the "New Disciplines." These are the programs that come wrapped in rhetoric about motivation and responsibility, dignity and cooperation and self-esteem. Look carefully at the pre-scriptions in the books and videos that describe these programs, and you will find a striking resemblance to standard old-time discipline.

The need to look carefully at such programs—and at the infor-mal classroom management practices that teachers use—is what led me to write this book. In fact, to be perfectly honest, I am suspicious of the very *word* "discipline"—perhaps because of its proximity to "bondage." I am even less enamored of the phrase "classroom man-agement." I remember using the latter term one day while chatting with my wife, who is not an educator. She interrupted me and echoed the phrase: "Classroom *management?*" Her tone was faintly incredulous, at once amused and appalled, and suddenly I saw an entire field as if for the first time.

*manager        managed*

"Management" is a term borrowed from business, of course, with overtones of directing and controlling employees. Like "discipline," it seems relevant to "groups of strangers rather than to people who are working together as a community" (Goodman 1992, p. 95; also see Bowers and Flinders 1990). In fact, the uncritical use of such terms reflects a willingness to accept some troubling assumptions about the relative roles and rights of those who are managing vis-à-vis those who are managed.

The fact that classroom management systems rarely prove satisfactory over the long run—hence the insatiable hunger for new techniques—should lead us to reconsider the whole enterprise of managing children. Thus, I want to invite educators to move beyond "discipline" or "management." I want to offer alternatives to the conventional goals and methods of discipline rather than another set of techniques for maintaining order.

Even those readers willing to join me in such an expedition may immediately demand to know whether they will be given a "practical alternative" to existing discipline programs. The answer is that it depends on how we want to define those words. On one level, I would reply: Yes. My purpose is not just to criticize the status quo but to move beyond it, not merely to interpret and analyze but to offer a framework that can help teachers and administrators change what they do.

But whenever I hear teachers ask for something they can "use," something that "works," I want to ask: Use for what? Works to accomplish what goal? Someone who has accepted uncritically the *objective* of discipline programs—namely, to get students to comply with whatever the adult demands—may insist that any alternative has to achieve the same end. Thus, anything that doesn't look, feel, and smell like a discipline program is, by definition, impractical.

Related to this is the desire for how-to guides: "When a student does such and such, tell me where to stand and how to look and what to say." This is the sort of demand that keeps classroom management consultants in business. But these easy-to-follow recipes are fundamentally insulting to teachers, not unlike attempts to design a "teacher-proof" curriculum. They are short-term fixes, instruments of control intended, at best, to stop bad behaviors rather than affirmatively help children to become good people.

After raising such questions about existing discipline programs and the very idea of discipline, I do lay out an alternative vision—one brought to life in those extraordinary classrooms I've visited. This alternative is neither a recipe nor a different technique for getting mindless compliance. It requires that we transform the classroom, give up some power, and reconsider the way we define and think about misbehavior. But despite those things—or, actually, *because* of those things—I believe it is exquisitely practical. In fact, it may be the only way to help children grow into caring and responsible adults.

My argument is that our first question should be "What do children need?"—followed immediately by "How can we meet those needs?"—and that from this point of departure we will end up in a very different place than if we had begun by asking, "How do I get children to do what I want?"

My argument is that how students act in school is so bound up with what they are being asked to learn as to raise serious questions about whether classroom management can reasonably be treated as a separate field.

My argument is that the quest to get students to act "appropriately" is curiously reminiscent of the quest to get them to produce the right answers in academic lessons. Thus, the constructivist critique, which says that a right-answer focus doesn't help children become good thinkers, also suggests that a right-behavior focus doesn't help children become good people.

I say that these are "my" arguments, but the truth is that I can't take credit for any of them—or for the details of application offered in the chapters that follow. More people than I can acknowledge have helped me to shape a vision of what schools might look like. I have in mind people like Dewey and Piaget, but also Marilyn Watson, Eric Schaps, and their colleagues at the Developmental Studies Center; Constance Kamii and Rheta DeVries and Lilian Katz; Rich

Ryan and Ed Deci at the University of Rochester; the late John Nicholls; and a lot of other educators and researchers committed to creating more democratic, collaborative schools.

I'm also indebted to the children and adults I've worked with over the years: students in my own classrooms, participants in my workshops (especially those who made me question my assumptions and practices), and teachers and administrators who let me into their classrooms and schools so I could watch. Naturally, none of these individuals, including those named above, should be held responsible for anything you are about to read. Just because they've had an impact on my thinking doesn't mean they would agree with my every thought.

Then there are the people who directly contributed to the book itself. Ron Brandt surely didn't have to throw his weight behind a project so controversial, but he did, and I'm grateful. Thanks also to Julie Houtz for her painstaking editing, and to the others on the ASCD staff who supported the book's production in various ways. Finally, I owe a giant debt of gratitude to the folks who have taken the trouble to read this book in manuscript form and offer their criticisms and suggestions: Bill Greene (who never fails me in this capacity and never fails to amaze me with the cogency of his comments), Alisa Kohn (who never fails to amaze me, period), Lisa Lahey, and Cynthia McDermott.

∞

# Chapter 1

# THE NATURE
# OF CHILDREN

The evidence increasingly points to an innate disposition [in children] to be responsive to the plight of other people. . . . Creating people who are socially responsive does not totally depend on parents and teachers. Such socializing agents have an ally within the child.

—Martin Hoffman (1986)

∞

## SELF-CENTERED AND POWER-DRUNK

Every teacher has a theory. Even the educator who cares only about practical strategies, whose mantra is "Hey, whatever works," is operating under a set of assumptions about human nature, about children, about that child sitting over there, about why that child did what she did just now. These assumptions color everything that happens in classrooms, from the texts that are assigned to the texture of casual interactions with students.

Despite their significance, such theories are rarely made explicit. No one comes out and says, "The reason I run the class this way is because I assume children are basically untrustworthy." But precisely because they have such a profound impact on every aspect of education, it is crucial to expose these beliefs and decide whether they can survive careful scrutiny. By the same token, whenever a consultant on discipline offers advice, we should hold that prescription up to

1

the light, much as we might search for a hidden watermark on a sheet of paper. What is he or she assuming about kids—and, by extension, about all people?

In particular, we need to be on the lookout for profoundly negative theories about the motives and capabilities of children, which frequently animate discussions about classroom management. Let's consider the hidden premises of some familiar assertions.

**"If the teacher isn't in control of the classroom, the most likely result is chaos."** Counterposing control to chaos, apart from calling up memories of the television series *Get Smart,* has the effect of ruling out any other possibilities. But this isn't an error in logic so much as it is a statement about one's view of the people in the classroom. It says that students—or perhaps humans in general—must be tightly regulated if they are to do anything productive. Notice that this doesn't merely speak to the value of having some *structure* to their activities; it says that external *control* is necessary, and without it, students are unlikely to learn or to act decently.*

**"Children need to be told exactly what the adult expects of them, as well as what will happen if they don't do what they're told."** These twin assumptions, both corollaries of the preceding one, are staples of the classroom management field. They speak volumes about the orientation of the person who holds them. They hint of disaster if students are asked to reflect on how they should conduct themselves instead of simply being told. They suggest that even broad guidelines are insufficient; what is necessary are precise instructions on how to behave. They imply that requests and explanations never suffice, that reasonable expectations won't be honored without threats of punishment. The kind of people for whom these things are true would not be much fun to spend time with, which may help to explain the way folks who hold these beliefs tend to act around children.

---

* It is theoretically possible that someone who believes this might add that it's true mostly because of what has been done to students up until now. The more common assumption, however, is that this is just the way kids are.

**"You need to give positive reinforcement to a child who does something nice if you want him to keep acting that way."** This common defense of praise seems to imply that the only reason a child would ever demonstrate kindness is to be rewarded with the approval of an adult. To talk about the need to "reinforce" a behavior suggests that the behavior would disappear in the absence of that reinforcement. Orthodox behaviorists believe this is true of everything. Lots of educators seem to believe it's true specifically of helpful acts. If qualities like generosity must be propped up by verbal rewards, they must be unnatural, which is to say that human beings left on their own are concerned only about themselves.

**"At the heart of moral education is the need to help people control their impulses."** The virtue of self-restraint—or at least the decision to give special emphasis to it—has historically been preached by those with a decidedly dark view of human nature, from Saint Augustine to the present day. In fact, at least three assumptions seem to be at work here: first, that we are all at war with ourselves, torn between our desires and our reason (or social norms); second, that these desires are fundamentally selfish, aggressive, or otherwise unpleasant; and third, that these desires are very strong, constantly threatening to overpower us.

What goes by the name of "character education" has enjoyed something of a resurgence in the mid-1990s, and we would do well to understand just what beliefs about human nature are driving the movement, or at least some of its most prominent advocates. Give them credit for candor, anyway; there is no need to speculate about hidden assumptions here. A "comprehensive approach [to character education] is based on a somewhat dim view of human nature," acknowledges William Kilpatrick (1992, p. 96). That view includes the assumptions that "the 'natural' thing to do in most situations is to take the easy way out" (p. 25) and that "most behavior problems are the result of sheer 'willfulness' on the part of children" (p. 249). "Character education . . . sees children as self-centered," says Kevin Ryan (1989, p. 16) and, according to Edward Wynne (1989, p. 25), is grounded in the work of theorists who share a "somewhat pessimistic view of human nature."

3

Mainstream writings on discipline differ from the dominant approach to character education mostly in that the former rarely own up to being based on a dim view of human nature. But here's what they do say:

- "'Working independently' is a euphemism" for higher rates of disruption and time off task. "In other words, while the cat's away, the mice will play" (Jones 1979, p. 30).
- "When [students] succeed in littering or in writing on walls, they feel encouraged to challenge other, more sacred, rules like the prohibition against assaulting fellow students" (Toby 1993/94, p. 8).
- "Children are not innately motivated to behave in school" (Canter and Canter 1992, p. 7). (See Appendix 2.)
- Does offering a reward for compliance constitute a bribe? "Sure—that's how motivation operates. . . . When people cooperate with us, they do what we want because doing so serves their purposes in some way" (Bluestein 1988, p. 117).[1]
- Without the "powerful reinforcement" of recognition, "students will likely revert to less cooperative ways" (Albert 1992a, p. 93).

The last declaration is offered as part of a program called Cooperative Discipline, whose author's favorite metaphor for describing students is that they dangle a rope in front of teachers, trying to lure us into an unproductive conflict. We must learn not to take the bait, which is to say we must resist the basic inclination of children (namely, to interrupt the learning process). Elsewhere in this program, we are introduced to a 1st grader who "just can't seem to concentrate" on his assignments even though he "can sit in the block corner for hours." The author's description of the child reads, in its entirety: "What a powerful manipulator!" (Albert 1989, p.47).

Rudolf Dreikurs, whose theories and techniques have been incorporated into a number of popular discipline programs, observed that "every educator's approach to the educational process is based on a certain concept of human nature" (Dreikurs, Grunwald, and Pepper 1982, p. 8). His own concept was, to a significant extent, borrowed from the psychology of Alfred Adler. Along with some dubious claims about the significance of birth order,[2] Adler offered a

4

theory of behavior as fundamentally goal-directed, and he argued that social interest, a desire to belong, is a central human goal. At times, Dreikurs seemed to endorse a benign view of children consistent with this Adlerian principle, saying that misbehavior represents a misguided attempt to feel significant and that kids who make trouble are mostly just discouraged.

But when Dreikurs and his associates began to address specific scenarios in homes and classrooms, their comments reflected a remarkably different view of children and their motives. In case after case, Dreikurs attributed anything that went wrong in a classroom to a child's unreasonable demand for attention. Thus, he argued, adults should never give a child attention "when he is seeking it" (Dreikurs and Cassel 1972, p. 36).[3]

Dreikurs's second favorite explanation for inappropriate behavior was the child's drive for power or superiority. Apparently, the possibility never occurred to him that a struggle to come out on top might be initiated by an adult, or that the child's need for power may reflect the objective situation of powerlessness that students usually face. Dreikurs's world was one populated by "power-drunk children" (Dreikurs and Grey 1968, p. 55) and defiantly "inattentive students" (p. 134). Doodling on desks is the act of "destructive children" (p. 162); if 1st graders come to blows, it is just because kids of that age "love to fight" (p. 154). Students who are late (p. 108) or fail to "heed instructions or to carry out assignments are doing this to get attention or want to show their power to do anything they want without anyone stopping them" (p. 193).

Dreikurs was disgusted by "the lengths to which children will go when they pretend to read but actually refuse to do so" (Dreikurs 1968, p. 152). He even remarked that "there is only a quantitative difference between . . . the 'normal' American child . . . [who] does not take a bath, refuses to do his homework, and so on . . . [and] the juvenile delinquent, who is openly at war with society" (Dreikurs 1968, p. 6). Adler's contention that children have a basic need to be part of a group became, in Dreikurs's hands, not reassurance about their motives but an invitation to rely on peer pressure as a way of controlling nonconformists (see Chapter 4). And a child who "resent[s] being discussed by the class" in this way was written off as someone who usually "takes all rights for himself and never grants the same rights to others. Often this child has serious behavioral problems" (Dreikurs et al. 1982, p. 167).[4]

Not long ago, an elementary principal in Wisconsin whose staff had been trained in the "STEP" program, a Dreikurs derivative, explained to me the philosophy they had adopted: "Kids have reasons for misbehaving and the idea is not to give them what they want." At the time, having accepted on faith what others had told me about the value of Dreikurs's work, I viewed her summary as an almost comical misreading of what she had been taught. Gradually, as I read that work for myself, I came to see that the problem lay less with her formulation than with the theory itself.

I linger on the views of Dreikurs—and, indeed, will return to his writings at several points in this book—because of the scope of his influence on contemporary educators. But the larger point here is not so much what he, or any other individual, believes. Rather, it is that we need to look carefully at what we are doing, and what classroom management theorists recommend, to determine the assumptions about children from which these practices emerge.

## AUSPICIOUS CIRCLES

We can often predict the way an adult will treat children simply from knowing what she believes about them. Someone who thinks that kids are always trying to get away with something is likely to believe that we adults must overcome these unsavory motives, force children to obey the rules, and see to it that they are punished when they don't. Indeed, research has shown that a dark view of human nature tends to be associated with controlling and punitive strategies (Clayton 1985). Truly, what we believe matters.

But even when an educator or consultant has nothing at all to say about the nature of children, his practices or prescriptions may speak for him. Because practice follows from theory, we can often derive theory from practice. Marilyn Watson has observed that discipline plans typically seem to proceed from the assumption that

6

Thomas Hobbes's famous characterization of life also applies to children: they are nasty, brutish, and short. One example of this, Watson continues, is the policy of arranging for students to experience what Dreikurs called "logical consequences." This practice is predicated on the disturbing and disrespectful assumption that children need to feel pain before they will stop behaving badly.[5] Something similar may be implicit in the very idea of "discipline" or classroom "management."

To take this idea another step, the practices that flow from a teacher's beliefs tend to elicit certain things from students. Label a particular child a troublemaker and watch him become one. View children in general as self-centered, and that is exactly the way they will come to act. Treat students "as if they need to be controlled" and you "may well undermine their natural predispositions to develop self-controls and internalized commitments to upholding cultural norms and values" (Watson 1984, p. 42).

Watch what happens when students escape temporarily from a teacher who thinks along these lines and has relied on tactics of control. When they are at lunch, in music or art class, on the bus, or in the hands of a substitute—in fact, whenever they are out of sight of the controller—the students may well explode. It doesn't take a degree in psychology to figure out that they may be trying to reclaim some of the autonomy that has been denied them.

But now notice what happens when this teacher discovers what has happened in her absence. Does she stop dead in her tracks and say to herself: "Whoa. I guess I need to take a hard look at these (negative) assumptions and (coercive) practices. Just look at the effect they're having"? Hardly. She announces triumphantly, "You see? You see what these kids are like? Give 'em an inch and they'll take a mile!" And she proceeds to respond with tighter control, tougher discipline, more coercion—and, above all, less trust.

The good news is that a more positive view of students has real-world consequences that are just as powerful. You may remember the so-called Pygmalion effect, documented in the 1960s, which showed that when teachers were led to believe that their students had extraordinary intellectual potential, these average students really did end up achieving impressively in their classes. Well, teachers who assume that children are capable of acting virtuously can likewise set into motion a self-fulfilling prophecy. They can create an "auspicious" circle rather than the more familiar vicious one. Thus, if a teacher trusts her students to make decisions, they will act very differently from those in her colleague's classroom if left on their own; typically, they will act responsibly and go right on with their learning (DeVries and Zan 1994, Hyman 1990).

This is compelling evidence that such a teacher is not just being naive or romantic in her assumptions, as the cynic may claim. (Of course, the cynic invariably denies being cynical and insists he is just being "realistic.") But what exactly does this more positive theory look like?

To reject a sour view of human nature, one predicated on the assumption that people are inherently selfish or aggressive, is not necessarily to assume that evil is illusory and everyone means well. We do not have to cast our lot with Carl Rogers—or Mr. Rogers, for that matter. Rather, we might proceed from the premise that humans are as capable of generosity and empathy as they are of looking out for Number One, as inclined (all things being equal) to help as to hurt.

Scores of studies from developmental and social psychology support exactly this conclusion and challenge the beliefs reviewed at the beginning of this chapter—that children will act generously only when reinforced for doing so, that people are motivated exclusively by self-interest, that students need to be controlled, and so on. Elsewhere, I have reviewed this literature in some detail (Kohn 1990a). For our purposes here, it may be enough to cite the conclusion of some of the leading researchers in the field of child development, whose own work at the National Institute of Mental Health confirms what other studies have found:

> Even children as young as 2 years old have (a) the cognitive capacity to interpret the physical and psychological states of others, (b) the emotional capacity to affectively experience the other's state, and (c) the behavioral repertoire that permits the possibility of trying to alleviate discomfort in others. These are the capabilities that, we believe, underlie children's caring behavior in the presence of another person's distress. . . . Young

8

children seem to show patterns of moral internalization that are not simply fear based or solely responsive to parental commands. Rather, there are signs that children feel responsible for (as well as connected to and dependent on) others at a very young age (Zahn-Waxler, Radke-Yarrow, Wagner, and Chapman 1992, pp. 127, 135).

When children do *not* act in a way consistent with these capacities, we might therefore come to a very different conclusion than that reached by the cynic. "Thoughtless" actions may be just what that word implies: attributable to a lack of thought, or skills. Children who act unkindly may be unaware of the effects of their actions on others, or unable to act otherwise. Carolyn Edwards (1986, pp. 40–41) offers the example of a group of four- and five-year-olds disparaging a three-year-old boy in their class who was physically as large as they were but, not surprisingly, lacked some of their skills. Were they being cruel? On the contrary, these children, given their level of cognitive development, were simply unable to understand that a child of their own size might not be as old, and thus as advanced in other respects.

Even older children may act in troubling ways because they are wanting for the sort of warm, caring relationships that enable and incline people to act more compassionately. They may have learned to rely on power rather than reason, to exhibit aggression rather than compassion, because this is what they have seen adults do—and perhaps what has been done to them. "Give 'em an inch and they'll take a mile" mostly describes the behavior of people who have hitherto been given only inches.

Our attention might well be focused on what children—and, by extension, adults—require for optimal functioning. Distilling a large quantity of psychological theory and research, Edward Deci and Richard Ryan (1990) have proposed three such universal human needs: autonomy, relatedness, and competence. Autonomy refers not to privacy but to self-determination, the experience of oneself as the origin of decisions rather than as the victim of things outside one's control. Relatedness means a need for connection to others, for belonging and love and affirmation. Finally, the presence of competence on this list suggests that all of us take pleasure from learning new things, from acquiring skills and putting them to use.[6]

I offer this list not as the last word on human needs, but as a reasonable beginning of such a discussion. Make up your own list, if you like. What matters is that our first questions about students are: What do they require in order to flourish? and How can we provide those things?—as opposed to, say, How can we make them do what we want? The implication of thinking along these lines is that if students disappoint us, it is almost always because they are missing something they need. While this way of framing the issue isn't quite the same as saying everyone is basically good, it is far more of a departure from the assumptions described earlier, the ones on which discipline plans so often rest.

The educator who takes to heart all these lessons about human nature doesn't assume that he can stand off to the side while children automatically grow into responsible adults. Rather, he models and explains and shows them he cares. He works with them so they will become better problem solvers and helps them see how their actions affect others. When children seem obnoxious, he is more inclined (depending on circumstances and the limits of his patience) to think in terms of providing guidance rather than enforcing rules. He views children who have trouble treating others with care or respect as needing help, just as children who have trouble solving math problems need help.

Furthermore, he is likely to follow the advice of Nel Noddings and attribute to students the best possible motive consistent with the facts (also see Molnar and Lindquist 1989). He knows we are most likely to help students develop good values by assuming whenever possible that they were already motivated by these values—rather than ascribing an ambiguous action to a diabolical desire to make trouble. He challenges himself and his colleagues to think twice before pigeonholing a particular student as a behavior problem or attributing sinister motives to children in general.

And he does what he can to help students create a sense of community in the classroom, to construct a place where they feel trusted and respected and empowered. We will return to these ideas

10

in later chapters after looking closely at more traditional discipline programs. For now it is enough to realize that these programs tend to be associated with a jaded view of children and human nature, and that a more optimistic perspective is both more accurate and more likely to generate practices that work.

∞

# Chapter 2

# BLAMING THE KIDS

To focus on discipline is to ignore the real problem: We will never be able to get students (or anyone else) to be in good order if, day after day, we try to force them to do what they do not find satisfying.

—WILLIAM GLASSER, *CONTROL THEORY IN THE CLASSROOM*

∞

## WHAT ARE WE ASKING?

Pick a book on discipline from your shelf and take a few minutes to leaf through it. Or, if you prefer, watch one of the countless videos on the subject that are now available, or sit in on a workshop. One way or another, you'll be treated to a bushel of suggestions for how to get students to behave however you want them to—or for how to get them to act "appropriately," which often amounts to the same thing. What you almost certainly will *not* find in any discipline program, however, is an invitation to reflect on what it is you want and whether it's reasonable.

People who market discipline programs know that it is deeply unsettling for educators to have to reconsider their requests and demands, their expectations and rules. It is far more convenient to take these things for granted, to treat them collectively as our point of departure so that we can concentrate on getting compliance. We prefer to avoid questions about the ends and instead focus on the means—which is to say, on techniques. Thus, *the problem always rests with the child who doesn't do what he is asked, never with what he has been asked to do.*

Some writers and consultants ensure this rather comfortable arrangement by offering theories to account for children's misbehavior that permanently locate the source of the problem—any problem—inside the student. For example, Rudolf Dreikurs insists that misbehavior can be explained by appealing to a fixed set of goals that he attributes to children, but that the children themselves are never aware of. These goals are: a quest for attention, power, revenge, and a desire to "display inadequacy" (or "use disability as an excuse") (Dreikurs 1968, pp. 27–32; Dreikurs and Grey 1968, pp. 36–40; Dreikurs et al. 1982, pp. 14–16). I've already suggested that these characteristics reflect a rather dark view of children. More than that, though, their effect is to circumvent anything like an open-minded attempt to make sense of what is going on in a classroom. Such an exploration would require us to entertain the possibility that it may be the teacher's request, rather than the child's unwillingness to comply with it, that needs to be addressed.

When one student punches another, of course, there isn't much controversy: almost all of us would agree that aggression should be condemned and stopped. But in more general terms, the crux of the matter may be who decides, and by what criteria, that a child's behavior *is* "misbehavior" in the first place. That inconvenient question, in turn, raises some others: Is a silent classroom really more conducive to learning than one where children are talking—or is it simply less trouble for the teacher? Is it reasonable to expect children to sit still for extended periods of time? Is it necessary for them to raise their hands before speaking, to keep their eyes on the teacher, to line up before leaving the classroom?

To anyone familiar with programs like Assertive Discipline, it will come as no surprise that such questions are never raised. Indeed, teachers are explicitly discouraged from reflecting on the wisdom of anything they are doing since this only produces "guilt, anxiety, and frustration" rather than "lead[ing] to confident behavior management" (Canter and Canter 1992, p. 9). The assertive teacher "tells students exactly what behavior is acceptable. . . . No questions. No room for confusion" (p. 27). This matter-of-fact demand for mindless obedience follows quite naturally from the premise that all problems are the students' fault. They are the ones who "talk when asked to be quiet; who dawdle when asked to work; who argue and talk back when asked to follow directions" (p. 6).

The creators of a rival program called Discipline with Dignity rightly observe that Assertive Discipline "sees students as the cause of all problems, so there are no demands on anybody else in the system to change" (Curwin and Mendler 1989, p. 83). But this criticism could well be leveled against their own approach. We are advised that the "effective" teacher in Discipline with Dignity might announce to a child, "Mary, we* raise our hands before speaking," followed ominously by "This is your reminder" (Curwin and Mendler 1988, p. 72). (In Assertive Discipline, the preferred word in the follow-up sentence is "warning"; otherwise, the two tactics are identical.) The rule in a 1st grade classroom, meanwhile, is that during story time, "Legs will be crossed, arms folded, and there will be no moving around once you sit" (p. 61). In neither of these examples do the authors consider that the rule itself might be problematic; rather, the rule is accepted without question and the task at hand is to impose a consequence on a student who persists in failing to obey.

It's much the same in a program called 21st Century Discipline (Bluestein 1988, p. 71), where teachers are essentially given a blank check: what matters, the reader is told, is

> what YOU want. Do you require a certain heading on the papers they turn in? Do you want them to push in their chairs before they leave the room? Will it drive you crazy if someone starts to sharpen a pencil while you are addressing the group? Where do you want the counters kept when the students are finished with them?

---

*The common use of the first person in such examples is disingenuous in the extreme since the speaker is exempt from whatever is required of "us." The teacher, of course, does not have to raise her hand.

Once again, there is not a whisper of inquiry into whether these are reasonable demands, or how it must feel to be a student in a place where one's own preferences don't count for much. Interestingly, this same author later recounts an episode in which a boy was not only eager to run an errand to the office but in fact "would do anything to get out of the room" where she was teaching. Rather than reflecting on what this might say about the kind of classroom she had created, the author merely pounces on the possibility of using such errands as rewards to control the student's future behavior (pp. 115–116).

The failure to examine our own actions and values is also reflected in other ways. In 1993, the National Association of Independent Schools sent out surveys to administrators, asking about moral issues they had dealt with. Of 130 surveys returned, only 9 mentioned anything about the values or actions of adults: for 93 percent of the respondents, to raise concerns about moral issues was almost by definition to focus on what children were doing wrong (Palma 1994).

Even if our only concern was to arrive at a more accurate assessment of what is really happening in a classroom, we would need to look hard at what we're asking students to do—and why. The Latin question "Cui bono?"—Who benefits?—should never be far from our minds: In whose interest is it to require students to do this or prohibit them from doing that? The temptation, of course, is to reply instantly that whatever we're demanding is for the children's own good. That's what a 6th grade teacher in northern California said when I asked her why she insisted on sharpening her students' pencils for them: left on their own, she declared, these kids will just grind the things down to little stumps.[1] A child in this classroom who believed herself capable of sharpening her own pencil, and did so, would have had to be disciplined since she had "misbehaved" according to the person with the power.

In this example, you or I might suspect that the problem is less the child's disobedience than the teacher's lack of trust or need for control; to think that an 11-year-old cannot handle this task is absurd. The trick, however, is to apply that same sharp scrutiny to our own beliefs and requirements. We need to be tough on ourselves in each instance and ask whether what we're demanding is truly necessary or productive, fair or age-appropriate. That means resisting the impulse to respond reflexively by reaching for some gimmick, whether home-grown or purchased from experts, to get students to fall in line. In other words, it means questioning the very premise of classroom management programs.

## HOW DOES THE CLASSROOM FEEL?

But assume that what we're requesting of students has passed the reasonability test and met the Cui Bono standard. Assume we're talking about an expectation as basic as honesty, and a problem as troubling as lying. Even here I think we have to summon the courage to look at the climate and structure of the classroom and ask whether these may have something to do with the action that disturbs us.

Why do people lie? Usually because they don't feel safe enough to tell the truth. The challenge for us is to examine that precept in terms of what is going on in our classroom, to ask how we and the students together might examine what underlies the lie, and figure out how we can make sure that even unpleasant truths can be told and heard. Does this mean fibbing is acceptable? No. It means the problem has to be dissected and solved from the inside out. It means behaviors occur in a context that teachers have helped to establish; therefore, teachers have to examine and consider modifying that context, even at the risk of some discomfort to themselves.

Contrast this approach with the two major variants of conventional discipline: the Old School insists that we must punish the liar, while the New School counsels gentleness as we try to figure out how to get the student to change his (dishonest) behavior. Is the latter approach preferable? No question about it. But ultimately the two are more similar than different because in both schools the blame rests entirely with the student.

Of course, no one uses the word *blame*. There's no need, when certain code words will do the job: we're told that the student who lies must be "held accountable"[2] or forced to "take responsibility" for the action he "chose." More generally, "everything [children] do is by their own decision. . . . Nobody makes them do anything, since they themselves decide what they will or will not do" (Dreikurs et al. 1982, p. 174; also see Charney 1991, p. 95).

Thus, in Cooperative Discipline, "all students are held accountable for all their actions . . . allowing no 'wiggle room' for escaping personal responsibility" (Albert 1992a, p. 85). A transparency master for this program features an illustration of a girl with her hands on her hips, wearing a self-satisfied smile and a ribbon pinned to her chest—while another student sits unhappily, arms folded, at a desk. The large caption reads: CONCEPT NUMBER 1: STUDENTS CHOOSE THEIR BEHAVIOR.

We will return (in Chapter 4) to the ways that the concept of choice is used, and misused, in discipline programs. For now, it is enough to notice that "choice" here does not signify a prescription for a democratic classroom, one in which students help to determine what happens. Rather, it is offered (without evidence)[3] as a *description*: Why don't students do what they're told? Because they choose not to.

Adults who blithely insist that children choose to misbehave are rather like politicians who declare that people have only themselves to blame for being poor. In both cases, potentially relevant factors other than personal responsibility are ignored. A young child in particular may not have a fully developed capacity for rational decision making or impulse control that is implicit in suggesting he made a choice. Teachers who think in terms of a lack of skills would be inclined to respond by trying to help the child develop these faculties, rather than by punishing and blaming. Indeed, two researchers recently discovered that the more teachers resorted to saying that a child simply "chose" to act inappropriately, the more likely they were to use punishment and other power-based interventions (Scott-Little and Holloway 1992).

Both educators and politicians are also the very people who benefit most from the claim that people's own choices determine what happens to them. The teacher who invokes the idea of choice has no need to reconsider her own decisions and demands. In the Cooperative Discipline illustration, we are discouraged from asking why the children have been set against each other in a race for artifi-cially scarce rewards, or what the long-term effects of that practice may be on their attitudes about themselves or each other or the task itself, or how other features of the classroom may have contributed to a child's failure. Teachers can simply tell themselves that a student "chose" whatever happened. No questions; no room for confusion.

Thus, that 6th grade teacher might well be able to point to exam-ples where her students had turned healthy pencils into piles of wood shavings and graphite dust. What she may have missed is the way her own mistrustful posture elicited precisely the kind of un-trustworthy behavior she predicted, and her tight control just called forth the "need" for more control. We have already become ac-quainted with the self-fulfilling prophecy. The point here is that when kids play fast and loose with the sharpener—or with the truth—our first question should not be "What do I do to make them stop?" but "What's happening here?" And, even though the answer will often lead us away from the classroom, perhaps into the home, teachers nevertheless would do well to follow that question with another: "Is it possible that decisions I've made and things I do might have some relation to what's happening here?"

## WHAT'S THE TASK?

If discipline programs studiously refrain from exploring whether an adult's request was reasonable and, more generally, how the envi-ronment created by the adult might have contributed to a student's response, their most salient omission must surely be the curriculum. A huge proportion of unwelcome behaviors can be traced to a prob-lem with what students are being asked to learn.*

The easiest problem to spot is that the tasks they've been given are so simple as to be boring—or, more commonly, too difficult (at least for a given child). It's hard for someone to admit she isn't smart

---

*Needless to say, it isn't always classroom teachers who are doing the asking. Mandates handed down from state legislatures, school boards, and administrators may be at the root of the problem. Whatever the source, though, the point is that to make sense of how students act we have to look hard at the curriculum.

enough to succeed at something; it's a great deal easier to displace that fear of being a failure, or to noisily distract oneself and others from the cause of the problem. Any number of perceptive teachers can tell stories about a student who stopped misbehaving as soon as something happened that made him feel competent: an easier task was presented, or he got help, or he was given more freedom to choose his tasks. And there is empirical research to support the conclusion that "when behavior problems arise in the classroom, one of the first factors to be examined should be instructional procedures and materials and their appropriateness for the offending student" (Center, Deitz, and Kaufman 1982, p. 371).[4]

Unfortunately, the curricular problems connected to troublesome behavior often go well beyond the difficulty level of assignments. Let's be honest: students frequently perceive the tasks they are given as not worth doing—and sometimes with good reason. Worksheets and textbooks and lectures are often hard to justify pedagogically. Even an assignment that could in principle be worthwhile may fail to engage students because its meaning and relevance were never explained, or because students had nothing to say about how it was to be done.

One of my own major (albeit belated) revelations as a teacher was that behavior problems in my classroom were not due to students' unnatural need for attention or power. The students were acting up mostly to make the time pass faster. And given the skills-based, decontextualized tasks I was assigning, who could blame them? Back then, I was thinking about a new approach to discipline. What I really needed was a new curriculum.

How do we work with students to create a meaningful curriculum that stretches their thinking, elicits their curiosity, and helps them reflect more skillfully on questions that are already important to them? To some extent, this question contains part of its answer. But the full response that it deserves would take us well beyond the scope of this book. Here the point isn't to describe the model of learning or the kind of tasks that might reduce behavior problems; it's merely to suggest that there is a connection. *When students are "off task," our first response should be to ask, "What's the task?"*

19

That response, however, is rarely heard within the field of classroom management. The point, remember, is to get compliance, to figure out what is wrong with the child who has failed to do an assignment, and then change that behavior. Even "non-disruptive off-task behavior is unacceptable and must be dealt with correctly" (Canter and Canter 1992, p. 163). You will not be surprised to learn that dealing with it "correctly" never seems to require the teacher to think about the assignment itself.

In Cooperative Discipline, much is made of enhancing children's self-esteem, which is said to derive in part from helping them feel "capable." But this, a video for the program quickly adds, means "capable of completing the academic tasks that we require of them" (Albert 1992b). Programs of classroom management rarely betray any awareness of, much less commitment to, the sort of learning that could be called constructivist or learner-centered. The examples of learning tasks they use are inadvertently revealing, tending toward individual seatwork involving reading textbooks (Canter and Canter 1992, pp. 133–134), completing worksheets and quizzes (Albert, 1989, p. 23), and answering questions such as "Who can tell me what the square root of 16 is?" (Curwin and Mendler 1988, p. 99).

Or consider this passage from Rudolf Dreikurs:

> One has to be careful with children who have little or no interest in the assigned classwork. In such cases, allowing them to do what they want may be only an invitation to avoid doing what they are supposed to do (Dreikurs and Grey 1968, p. 192).

This position seems to suggest that one doesn't have to be careful with one's assignments—only with those darned kids who have the nerve to find them uninteresting. The relevant criterion has nothing to do with learning but with doing what one is "supposed to do" (as determined unilaterally by the person in control). One searches in vain here for a real departure from Canter (1988, p. 73), who apparently regards "on-task time" and "learning" as interchangeable concepts.

All of this may be objectionable if only for its fundamentally conservative posture: to take the academic status quo for granted is to perpetuate it. But it also offers a clue to the inherent limits of such an approach. How students act in class is so intertwined with curricular content that *it may be folly even to talk about classroom management or discipline as a field unto itself.* That is a subversive sentence: taken seriously, it has the potential to subvert the entire field. But how can we deny that the way children act in a classroom is significantly related to their interest in what they've been given to do? Tapping and extending that interest takes time and talent, patience and skill and even courage (in being willing to take a hard look at one's curriculum). Small wonder there is more demand for strategies to get kids to Just Do It.

To put this discussion back in perspective, the curriculum is part of the larger classroom context from which any student's behavior, or misbehavior, emerges. An authentic response to the behavior calls upon us to examine the whole of that context and consider changing it. The failure to do so amounts to blaming the student—which, in turn, gives rise to the familiar tactics of manipulation discussed in the next chapter.

∝

# Chapter 3

# BRIBES AND THREATS

> If you punish a child for being naughty, and reward him for being good, he will do right merely for the sake of the reward; and when he goes out into the world and finds that goodness is not always rewarded, nor wickedness always punished, he will grow into a man who only thinks about how he may get on in the world, and does right or wrong according as he finds of advantage to himself.
>
> —IMMANUEL KANT, *EDUCATION*

∞

Once we have reassured ourselves that virtually all problems in a classroom are the fault of the students, and once we have decided that our role is mostly to "manage" their behavior until it becomes acceptable to us, there are remarkably few practical options available. The cards to be played, so to speak, have already been dealt. That is why the methods outlined in discipline programs typically amount to variations on two or three basic themes. These themes, moreover, are just as pervasive in classrooms where the teacher has never read a book or attended a workshop on classroom management; the formal programs just refine and systematize the application of these same interventions.

## COERCION

The most basic way to get what you want from someone, assuming you have more power than he does, is just to make him do it. Technique number one, then, is straightforward coercion: without regard to motive or context, past events or future implications, the adult simply forces the child to act (or stop acting) in a certain way.

- Problem: Chris and Pat, who are sitting next to each other, are making an unusual amount of noise. Maybe one is annoying the other, or maybe the two are simply talking together, oblivious to everything else going on in the room. Solution: The teacher points to one of the students and then to a distant chair. "Chris, sit over there."*
- Problem: Petrified clumps of chewing gum are appearing under tables and desktops throughout the school. Solution: Ban the stuff. The adult in charge simply decrees that there will be no more gum chewing in school.
- Problem: Kids are coming to school in outrageous clothes, offensive to certain adults or perhaps just so expensive as to suggest that an elaborate status contest is underway. Solution: Tell students what they may and may not wear (dress code), or compel them all to wear the same thing (uniforms).

To make sense of this technique, and the ones that follow, it may help to consider the following framework. As educators, our responses to things we find disturbing, our approach to both academic and nonacademic matters, might be described as reflecting a philosophy of either doing things *to* students or working *with* them. As with any dichotomy, there are limits to this classification scheme. But I believe it is a useful exercise to take any of our policies and try to decide whether it more nearly resembles "doing to" or "working with." (Alternatively, one could start with these concepts and then try to think of real practices that exemplify them.)

In any case, simple coercion is the purest illustration of "doing to." The students in each of these examples are treated as objects

---

* Or perhaps, "Chris, you need to sit over there." The invocation of what someone "needs" to do usually has much less to do with that person's needs than with the preferences of the speaker.

rather than subjects. Adults decide unilaterally when there is a problem and what is to be done about it.

And the effect? Consider Chris and Pat. When the teacher separates them, does either student come away with any understanding of, or concern about, how his or her actions may affect other people in the room? Have the two learned how to negotiate a solution, attend to social cues, or make the best of sitting next to someone who is not a friend? Hardly. But they, like the other students watching, have learned one important lesson from this intervention. That lesson is power: when you have it (as the teacher does, at the moment), you can compel other people to do whatever you want.

## THE MEANING OF PUNISHMENT

The second major disciplinary technique is punishment, which is easy to confuse with coercion. Two features, however, have to be present for an intervention to qualify as a punishment: it must be deliberately chosen to be unpleasant, such as by forcing the student to do something he would rather not do or preventing him from doing something he wants to do; and it must be intended to change the student's future behavior. A punishment makes somebody suffer in order to teach a lesson.

Our predilection for euphemism has allowed us to avoid seeing punitive practices for what they are. Thus, we incarcerate students but describe it as "detention." We exile them from the community and refer to it as "suspension." We forcibly isolate small children and call it by the almost Orwellian name "time out." And then there is the most ambitious euphemism of all, which allows adults to punish children in any number of ways but describe what they are doing as merely imposing "logical consequences." (These last two labels are discussed in the next chapter.)

The techniques for punishing go on and on. We humiliate students by what we say to them in front of their peers. We send ominous notes home to parents. We withdraw privileges, which sometimes seem to have been dangled in front of students for the express purpose of being snatched away at our pleasure. We remand students to the principal's office, give them bad grades, saddle them with extra work, and even (in some states) resort to physical violence.

These punishments are not equivalent; some of them carry uniquely destructive effects. Corporal punishment, the worst of all, has long ago been renounced by most Western nations. As researchers have documented for decades, using force on children teaches them that aggression is acceptable, to say nothing of its other psychological effects (e.g., Straus 1994, Hyman 1990). Sending a student to the principal's office for punishment, meanwhile, tends to turn the principal into an ogre in the eyes of the students. Giving them additional (or longer) assignments when they have done something wrong sends a powerful message to everyone that learning is aversive, something one would never *want* to do.

Let's leave aside the specifics, though, and consider punishment as a category. Quite a few writers have cautioned that it does little good to threaten a punishment if the threat isn't credible, or to use one that isn't actually aversive to the recipient.[1] But assume we have punished "properly." When I address a group of educators or parents, I like to dramatically extract an imaginary gun from behind the podium, wave it around, and threaten to shoot anyone who talks during the presentation. I ask whether this threat will keep the room quiet, and of course, there is little doubt about the answer.

So: does punishment work? In this example, everyone finds the prospect of being shot sufficiently disagreeable, my aim is good, and I have been convincing about my willingness to pull the trigger. (I have had a *very* bad week.) The answer, then, is that punishment can be quite effective indeed—but only to get one thing: temporary compliance.

Reflect for a moment on the limits of such an accomplishment. Punishment generally works only for as long as the punisher is around. But this is not just because it loses effectiveness over time, like a medication. It's because the student is led to focus on avoiding the punishment itself. A child who hears "I don't want to catch you doing that again . . . or else!" may quite reasonably reply (if only to herself), "Fine. Next time you won't catch me."

Another way to put this is to say that punishment, even at its most successful, can only change someone's behavior. It can't possibly have a positive effect on that person's motives and values, on the person underneath the behavior. The fact that teachers continue to punish the same students over and over suggests that the problem with this strategy runs deeper than the way a particular punishment has been implemented.

## THE PRICE OF COMPLIANCE

Perhaps your response to these arguments is something like the following: "Hey, don't knock temporary compliance. When a student acts intolerably—when other kids are prevented from learning—I'll settle for whatever stops it."

My answer is threefold. First, if you have to keep returning to the same strategy, then it isn't particularly effective, even for a limited goal like stopping a particular behavior. Not long ago, a teacher told me how a colleague of hers had had enough of a student and, as she had so often done throughout the year, told him he was to report to the principal's office. In one of those moments of blistering clarity (for those ready to receive them), the boy turned to the teacher on his way out the door and said quietly, "This has never helped before. Why do you think it's going to help now?"

Second, punishment doesn't just fail to solve problems: it generally makes them worse. Researchers have found, for example, that children who are severely punished at home are *more* likely than their peers to act out when they are away from home. I have yet to find an educator who is surprised by this finding, which suggests that we have all noticed something similar going on in schools. The problem is that we have trouble acting on this recognition.

Several years ago, I spotted a sign taped to a wall in a 6th grade classroom in Idaho. It read: THE BEATINGS WILL CONTINUE UNTIL MORALE IMPROVES. The good news is that the sign was intended ironically. The bad news is that something similarly illogical underlies any use of punishment, even if the beatings are only figurative and regardless of whether the objective is to enhance morale or to achieve something else. The more you punish someone, the more angry that person becomes, and the more "need" there is to keep punishing. If this is not an example of a vicious circle, then that term has no meaning.

Finally, and perhaps most significantly, punishment creates a new set of problems, proving worse in many respects than doing nothing at all:

• **It teaches a disturbing lesson.** Like simple coercion, punishment models the use of power—as opposed to reason or cooperation—and this can profoundly affect a child's developing value structure. Specifically, the child learns that when you don't like the way someone is acting, you just make something bad happen to that person until he gives in: Do this or here's what I'm going to do to you. Much of what is disturbing about some children's behavior suggests that they have learned this lesson all too well—possibly from us.

• **It warps the relationship between the punisher and the punished.** Once an adult has come to be seen as an enforcer of rules and an imposer of unpleasant consequences, the child is about as happy to see that person coming as an adult is to see a police car in the rearview mirror. The caring alliance between adult and child, so vital to the latter's growth, has been significantly compromised.

This fact, by the way, also helps to explain why punishment typically exacerbates exactly what it is meant to improve. To help an impulsive, aggressive, or insensitive student become more responsible, we have to gain some insight into why she is acting that way. That, in turn, is most likely to happen when the student feels close enough to us (and safe enough with us) to explain how things look from her point of view. The more students see us as punishers, the less likely it is that we can create the sort of environment where things can change.

Imagine that Randy sticks out his foot just as Kenny is passing by his desk, causing Kenny to fall on his face. And imagine that the teacher punishes Randy by making him sit all alone in a room while everyone else is off doing something enjoyable. Let's look in on Randy and try to guess what's going through his mind. Maybe, as the teacher who punished him would like to think, he's reflecting on what he did, saying to himself thoughtfully, "Gee, now I understand that hurting people is wrong . . ."

Right. And maybe next year teachers will be paid as much as professional athletes.

Back in the real world, the chances are that Randy is angry and bitter, feeling picked on unfairly. He's blaming Kenny for his troubles and possibly planning a spectacular revenge at a time and place where he won't get caught. Also, he probably feels resentful of, and alienated from, the teacher who put him there. Don't expect him to come up to that teacher later, feeling a little embarrassed, and say, "I know it wasn't cool to trip him and stuff, and I feel kinda bad, but God, it's like Kenny is your favorite! It's like everything he does, he's Mr. Perfect. And that just makes me really mad, OK?"

Such an explanation doesn't excuse hurting someone, of course, but how can you expect to make any headway with Randy if you don't *know* that this is how he experiences the classroom? And how can you expect to know this if your relationship with him has been eroded as a result of defining yourself as a punisher? The point here, again, is that punishment shouldn't be avoided just because it's mean or disrespectful, but also because it makes it harder to solve problems.

• **Punishment actually impedes the process of ethical development.** A child threatened with an aversive consequence for failing to comply with someone's wishes or rules is led to ask, rather mechanically, "What do they want me to do, and what happens to me if I don't do it?"—a question altogether different from "What kind of person do I want to be?" or "What kind of community do we want to create?"

Think about such a shift in the context of this commonly heard defense of punishment:

> When children grow up and take their places in society, they're going to realize that there are consequences for their actions! If they rob a bank and get caught, they're going to be put in jail. They'd better learn that lesson right now.

The fatal flaw in this argument is that we want children not to rob banks—or do various other things that are unethical or hurtful—

28

because they know it's wrong, and also because they can imagine how such actions will affect other people. But when disciplinarians talk about imposing "consequences" for a student's action—and inducing him to think about those consequences ahead of time—they almost always mean the consequences *to him*. The focus is on how *he* will get in trouble for breaking the rule. This fact, so fundamental that it may have escaped our notice entirely, is a devastating indictment of the whole enterprise. Just as some people try to promote helping or sharing by emphasizing that such behaviors will eventually benefit the actor (see Kohn 1990a), so the reason for the child to behave "appropriately" is the unpleasantness he will suffer if he fails to do so.

By contrast, ethical sophistication consists of some blend of principles and caring, of knowing how one ought to act and being concerned about others. Punishment does absolutely nothing to promote either of these things. In fact, it tends to *undermine* good values by fostering a preoccupation with self-interest (McCord 1991). "What consequence will I suffer for having done something bad?" is a question that suggests a disturbingly primitive level of moral development, yet it is our use of punishment that causes kids to get stuck there!

You say you're concerned about the real world, where some people do awful things? So am I. In the real world, getting children to focus on what will happen to them if they are caught misbehaving simply is not an effective way to prevent future misbehavior because it does nothing to instill a lasting commitment to better values or an inclination to attend to others' needs. Most people who rob banks assume they won't get caught, in which case there will be no consequences for their action, which means they have a green light to go ahead and rob.

In fact, if an auditorium were filled with bank robbers, wife batterers, and assorted other felons, we would likely find, as Thomas Gordon (1989, p. 215) has remarked, that a significant majority of them were regularly punished as children.[2] They weren't encouraged to focus on how others were affected by what they were doing. They were trained to think about what would happen to them if some more powerful person, for any reason or no reason, didn't like it. In other words, the problem is more likely to be too much discipline than too little, at least as that word is typically used.[3]

# WHY WE PUNISH

So why do we do it? Why do we continue to rely on punishment if it makes things worse in the classroom (and elsewhere)? Here are some answers that make sense to me, many of which I've heard from educators around the country.

- It's quick and easy. Lots of thought and skill are required to work *with* students to figure out together how to solve a problem. There's no trick to just making something bad happen to a child who fails to do what we say.

- It obviously works to get temporary compliance, while its relation to the various long-term harms described here is harder to see. Result: it keeps getting used.

- Most of us were raised and taught in environments that were, to some degree, punitive, and we live what we know. Hence the phenomenon known as "How did my mother (or father or teacher) get in my larynx?" The flip side of this is that many of us don't know what else to do.

- It's expected by various constituencies: administrators, colleagues, and even the students themselves. From parents, we can often count on hearing, "What are you going to do to the kid who did this to my kid?" (This is an invitation for us to ask whether the goal is to get revenge or solve the problem.)

- It makes us feel powerful. A defiant student has issued a challenge that many adults feel obliged to answer by making sure they wind up on top. There's no better way to win the battle—and, indeed, this rationale implicitly assumes the existence of an adversarial encounter—than by using one's power to make the student unhappy. Thus, when that teacher was asked why she thought sending the student to the principal's office yet again was likely to help, the question may have been misconceived: perhaps it wasn't intended to help at all but simply to let that teacher feel triumphant. "I'm on top again; I'm back in control."

- It satisfies a desire for a primitive sort of justice, a rarely articulated but deep-rooted belief (at least, among some people) that if you do something bad, something bad should happen to you—regardless of the long-term practical effects.

- We fear that if students *aren't* punished, they will think they "got away with" something and will be inclined to do the same thing again—or worse. Apropos of Chapter 1, it's interesting to ponder the hidden beliefs about children, and about human nature, that animate this fear.

- Finally, punishment continues as a result of a false dichotomy—an unnecessary either/or—that is lodged in many of our brains. On the one hand, we can punish; on the other hand, we can do nothing, let it go, give the kid another chance. Thus, until we have made the wrongdoer suffer, we haven't really taken any action. We haven't gotten serious; we've been permissive, or "soft." Any attempt to get to the bottom of the problem by working with the student is therefore just a fancy version of doing nothing.

Once, in a workshop, as I laid out the arguments against punishment, I noticed a middle-aged man, a junior high school guidance counselor, starting to turn red with rage. Finally he could stand it no longer and shouted, "You're telling me if a kid comes up to me in the hall and calls me a son of a bitch, I'm supposed to *let it go!*"

Now, part of this man's reaction may have come from the need to triumph over the student, to show him who's boss. He might have been afraid that refraining from punishment would leave him feeling that the student had got the better of him. But at bottom I suspect that this counselor had made room in his head for two, and only two, possible responses: punitive action and inaction. If his repertoire was limited to these options, then there was no way other than punishment to communicate that what the student had said was unacceptable. Thus, not to punish is tantamount to losing one's only mechanism for making a judgment, one's only way of indicating that it's not OK to talk to someone like that. Until this false dichotomy (punishing versus doing nothing) is identified and eradicated, we cannot hope to make any progress in moving beyond punitive tactics.

Any of these reasons, then, might explain why we continue to punish. But none of them proves that it's necessary, much less desirable, to do so. None of them offers any reason to think that punishment is effective at helping students to become caring, responsible members of a community. And none of them changes the fact that the obedience produced by punishment comes at a terrible price.

# REWARDS

What if, instead of threatening my audience with a gun, I had offered them money for doing something? Suppose I had announced that I wanted everyone in the room to cross his or her legs, and that my assistants were clandestinely scattered throughout the room to monitor their compliance. (This is one of many things that punishments and rewards share: both require surveillance.) Keep your right leg on top of the left one until the session is over and you'll get $2,000, I tell them. Will they do it?

Someone would have to be awfully defiant, or awfully rich, to turn down such an offer. The question, then, is "Do rewards work?" And the answer should sound familiar: Sure! Rewards work very well to get one thing, and that thing is temporary compliance. The third technique of classroom management, alongside coercion and punishment, is dangling rewards in front of students for doing what we demand. Instead of "Do this—or here's what I'm going to do to you," we say, "Do this—and you'll get that." Instead of leading a student to ask herself "What do they want me to do, and what happens to me if I don't do it?", her question becomes "What do they want me to do, and what do I *get* for doing it?" The latter question, of course, is no closer to the kind of thinking we would like to promote.

"Do this and you'll get that" is at the heart of countless classroom management programs, including some that energetically promote themselves as positive or enlightened. These books can be summarized in four words: Punishments bad, rewards good. Although it is tempting to regard a strategy based on the use of carrots to get compliance as more humanistic than one based on sticks, these two approaches are far more similar than different. They are two sides of the same coin—and the coin doesn't buy very much.

Because I have written an entire book on the subject of rewards (Kohn 1993a), there isn't any need to rehearse all the arguments and evidence again here. Instead I will make just a few points to indicate why rewards belong in the category of things to move beyond.

The key to understanding why positive reinforcement isn't really so positive is to recognize the distinction between the goody itself and its status as a reward. It's the difference between money and merit pay, between having a popcorn party with your class and telling your class that they will get a popcorn party *if they're good this week*.

Carrots seem more desirable than sticks because people like getting carrots. Kids usually love the stickers and stars, the A's and praise, the parties and pizza and payments. But what no one likes is to have the very things he needs or desires used to manipulate his behavior. Rewards, in the unforgettable phrase of Edward Deci and Richard Ryan (1985, p. 70), are just "control through seduction." In the long run, control of any variety is aversive—and we should expect that, ultimately, rewards wouldn't work much better than punishments.

And as a matter of fact, they don't. At least two dozen studies have shown that when people are promised a reward for doing a reasonably challenging task—or for doing it well—they tend to do inferior work compared with people who are given the same task without being promised any reward at all. Other research has shown that one of the least effective ways to get people to change their behavior (quit smoking, lose weight, use their seatbelts, and so on) is to offer them an incentive for doing so. The promise of a reward is sometimes not just ineffective but counterproductive—that is, worse than doing nothing at all.

Most relevant to our subject here is the finding that children who are frequently rewarded tend to be somewhat less generous and cooperative than those who aren't rewarded (Fabes, Fultz, Eisenberg, May-Plumlee, and Christopher 1989; Grusec 1991; for other research, see Kohn 1990a, pp. 202–203). Some teachers and parents find that result shocking. Others understand it immediately: Rewards, like punishments, can only manipulate someone's actions. They do nothing to help a child become a kind or caring person.

In fact, what the rewarded child has learned is that if he is generous he will get something. When the goodies are gone, so is the inclination to help. By the same token, a student who does what we want in order to receive some reward can't really be described as "behaving himself." It would be more accurate to say that the reward is behaving him.

Some educators are genuinely concerned about helping students become caring people—and genuinely misguided in believing that a program in which the adults "catch children doing something right," and offer them the equivalent of a doggie biscuit, will help that to happen. It won't. But in lots of classrooms and schools, such reward-based programs aren't really intended to help students become "responsible" or "good citizens"; these are just code words for blindly following someone else's rules. The point is not altruism but compliance.

When rewards are used for the purpose of eliciting mindless obedience, it soon becomes clear just how similar they are to punishment. Another form of evidence comes from noticing that the teachers and principals who have a reputation for enjoying power and needing to be in control are often the people most enamored of behavior management systems that feature rewards and praise. This is not a coincidence; indeed, research has confirmed a link between a tendency to control and a reliance on praise (e.g., Deci, Spiegel, Ryan, Koestner, and Kauffman 1982).

But we don't need studies to tell us about this connection. All we may need to know is that rewards and praise play a central role in Assertive Discipline. "Positive recognition . . . must become the most active part of your classroom discipline plan," says Lee Canter (Canter and Canter 1992, p. 57).[4] For educators who recoil from a program as coercive as this one, yet have always assumed that positive recognition is beneficial, trying to reconcile these two ideas can be profoundly unsettling.

Educators who genuinely seek to help students become more excited about learning or more confident about their abilities should reflect carefully on what distinguishes the sort of positive feedback likely to have those effects from the sort that backfires (Kohn 1993a, chap. 6). If that distinction is sometimes murky in practice, there is one area where the damaging effects of praise ought not to be surprising, and that is where expressing approval is intended as a verbal reward—and, to that extent, as a way of manipulating students' future behavior.

Consider how many teachers gush over the way a child has acted, telling her how pleased or proud they are: "I like the way you found your seat so quickly and started working, Alisa!" The most important word in this sentence is *I*. The teacher is not encouraging Alisa to reflect on how she acted, to consider why one course of action might be better than another. Quite the contrary: all that counts is what the teacher wants, and approval and attention are made conditional on doing it. Truly, this sort of praise is not about bolstering self-esteem; it is about "control through seduction." No wonder it is an integral part of the same discipline programs that include punishment.

Things get even worse when such comments are offered in front of others (e.g., Canter and Canter 1992, pp. 143–145): "I like the way Alisa has found her seat so quickly . . . " Here the teacher has taken rewards, which are bad enough, and added to them the poison of competition. Children are set against one another in a race to be the first one praised. This sort of practice does Alisa no favors; one can imagine how the other kids will treat her later: "Look, it's Miss Found-Her-Seat Dork!" Over time, singling children out like this works against any sense of community in the classroom.

What's more, public praise is a fundamentally fraudulent interaction in its own right. The teacher is pretending to speak to Alisa, but is actually *using* her, holding her up as an example in an attempt to manipulate everyone else in the room. Even apart from its long-term effects, this is simply not a respectful way to treat human beings. And needless to say, seeing a *group* of students used in this manner is just as disturbing (e.g., Slavin 1995, p. 135).

Similar to public praise in its divide-and-conquer approach is the use of collective rewards. Here the teacher holds out a goody to the whole class if everyone does what he demands, the point being to make the students pressure their peers to obey (Canter and Canter 1992, pp. 69–71; Jones 1979). Thus, the children become unwitting accomplices of the teacher, doing his dirty work for him. Should the teacher ultimately opt not to provide the goody, woe to the child who is regarded as the reason for this decision. Once again we glimpse the punitive underbelly of reward systems.

But these are only particularly egregious examples of what goes on whenever teachers make something—be it attention or food— conditional on students' compliance. Like punishments, rewards warp the relationship between adult and child. With punishments, we come to be seen as enforcers to be avoided; with rewards, as goody dispensers on legs. In neither case have we established a caring alliance, a connection based on warmth and respect. Like punishments, rewards try to make bad behaviors disappear through manipulation. They are ways of doing things *to* students instead of working *with* them.

Make no mistake: the issue is not which reward or punishment we use, or how such a program is implemented, or what criteria are used to decide who gets a goody or a consequence. Such questions occupy school faculties for meeting after meeting, and they are massive exercises in missing the point. The problem rests with the very nature of these basic tools of traditional discipline. For all the reasons discussed in this chapter, schools will not become inviting, productive places for learning until we have dispensed with bribes and threats altogether.

∞

# PUNISHMENT LITE: "CONSEQUENCES" AND PSEUDOCHOICE

> The would-be progressives . . . thought that there were good ways and bad ways to coerce children (the bad ones mean, harsh, cruel, the good ones gentle, persuasive, subtle, kindly), and that if they avoided the bad and stuck to the good they would do no harm. This was one of their greatest mistakes.
>
> —JOHN HOLT, *HOW CHILDREN FAIL*

∞

A growing number of educators are in the market, quite literally, for alternatives to the coercive, traditional kind of discipline. They have misgivings about programs in which adults are essentially urged to assert their will over children, to wield rewards and punishments until students obey without question. Many of these educators have eagerly signed up for new classroom management programs that bill themselves as more modern and humane.

One of the central purposes of this book, as you may have noticed by now, is to inquire whether these "New Disciplines," with names like Cooperative Discipline and Discipline with Dignity, represent a real departure from what they claim to replace. Whether we are talking about their view of human nature (Chapter 1), their assumptions about where the fault lies when things go wrong in

37

a classroom (Chapter 2), or what we are ultimately trying to achieve (Chapter 5), there is reason to believe that these programs are different only in degree, rather than in kind, from the more traditional approach. Notwithstanding the rhetoric they employ, the New Disciplines suggest a subtler, somewhat nicer way by which we can continue to do things *to* children—as distinct from working *with* them in a democratic environment to promote their social and moral development.[1]

# REWARDS REDUX

The first clue to the nature of the New Disciplines comes from the fact that many of these programs use rewards to control behavior, as described at the end of the last chapter. A glance at any book with "classroom management" in the title will confirm the pervasiveness of this approach. Dreikurs, to his credit, offered an incisive analysis of the dangers of praise, recommending in its place a kind of nonevaluative feedback that he called "encouragement" (Dreikurs et al. 1982, pp. 108–112; Dreikurs and Grey 1968, p. 57), although he sometimes seemed inconsistent on this point.[2] Some of the books derived from Dreikurs's work contain brief passages in which the idea of rewarding or praising children for being good is viewed with the appropriate skepticism (Nelsen 1987, p. 13; Albert 1989, p. 66).

Yet Cooperative Discipline, whose author's misgivings about rewards seem to be limited to the fact that children will keep demanding more of them, is peppered with Skinnerian gimmicks, such as handing out "stars and stickers . . . [and] awards" (Albert 1989, pp. 102, 111), writing the names of well-behaved students on the chalkboard (p. 38), publicly praising someone "who's on task" in order to get another student to comply (Albert 1995, p. 44), and even pinning ribbons on children (Albert 1992a, p. 38).

Likewise, Discipline with Dignity, far from "overlook[ing] the importance of positive reinforcement," as Canter (1988, p. 72) claims, fairly bubbles with enthusiasm about extrinsic inducements. These include a list of ten different "classroom privileges [that] should be earned, not given," such as field trips, free time, being a hall monitor, and so on (Curwin and Mendler 1988, p. 56). Also recommended: a "merit/demerit system to encourage successful cooperation"—which, moreover, is turned into a competition so that only "the table that most successfully worked together as a team gets a merit" (p. 59)—and exemptions from homework for good behavior (p. 78). Teachers are also urged to "catch a student being good" every few minutes and praise that child (p. 97)—a very specific echo of Assertive Discipline (e.g., Canter and Canter 1992, p. 60).[3]

# REPACKAGED PUNISHMENT

The New Disciplines may depend on rewards, but their central claim is that, unlike their old-fashioned counterparts, they reject the use of punishment. Sometimes sounding for all the world like William Glasser, Thomas Gordon, or Haim Ginott, the purveyors of these programs eloquently denounce the practice of punishing children, declaring that it "provokes hostility and antagonism" (Albert 1989, p. 79) and a desire "to get even very soon" (Nelsen 1987, p. 67), that it is "ineffective for long-term change" (Curwin and Mendler 1988, p. 69) and "outdated" (Dreikurs and Grey 1968, p. 47).

So far, so good. But the programs influenced by Dreikurs present as an alternative to punishment the idea of imposing "logical consequences" on children when they do something wrong. Logical consequences are said by various writers to differ from punishment in any of three basic ways: They are (1) motivated by a desire to instruct, (2) reasonable and respectful in their application, and (3) related to the act of the wrongdoer.

Before examining each of these criteria more closely, it's instructive to observe that even the people who have built their careers on the ostensible benefits of logical consequences sometimes acknowledge that what they are proposing can be pretty tough to distinguish from old-fashioned punishment. The authors of one discipline guide for parents (Dinkmeyer and McKay 1989, p. 85) admit that "the line between punishment and logical consequences is thin at times." Another writer (Albert 1989, p. 79) concedes that, after all, the message in both cases is essentially the same: "when you do this, then [that] will happen." And Dreikurs himself (Dreikurs and Grey 1968, p. 58) observed at one point that "tone of voice alone often distinguishes one from the other."

Another reason to question the distinction between punishment and logical consequences is supplied (inadvertently) by Assertive Discipline. In this program, the names of disobedient children are conspicuously recorded—and, later, checked off—on a clipboard.[4] This is quite simply a threat, since further misbehavior brings down on the child's head a variety of punishments, which have already been listed on the wall in order of severity. What's interesting for our purposes is that Canter explicitly disavows the label of punishment, preferring to refer to forcible isolation, a disapproving note to the child's parents, and a trip to the principal's office as—you guessed it—"consequences" (Canter and Canter 1992, p. 82).

Thomas Gordon, who devised the influential approach to working with children known as Parent Effectiveness Training (P.E.T.), was forced to conclude that "Dreikurs's concept of 'logical consequences' is . . . nothing less than a euphemism for external control by punishment; it's another act of punitive discipline" (Gordon 1989, pp. 31–32). But let's look more closely at the claim that there really is a difference between logical consequences and punishment. Many teachers and principals have signed up for New Discipline programs precisely because they have been promised a nonpunitive technique for getting student compliance.

First, users of Discipline with Dignity are informed that the recipient of a logical consequence "may feel lousy," but that "there's an instructional intent" to making him feel that way (Curwin and Mendler 1991, Part 2; also see 1988, p. 71). The problem here, of course, is that any punishment, regardless of its severity or negative effects, can be rationalized in exactly the same manner. Presumably, many of the "more than three million American children [who] are physically abused each year in the name of discipline" (Lewin 1995)[5] are told that punishment is necessary to "teach them a lesson" or is "for their own good."

Dreikurs offers a different version of this criterion, specifying the *nature* of the instructional intent. Whereas punishments underscore the authority of the adult doing the punishing, logical consequences are supposed to be geared to preserving the "social order" more generally, so that children "learn to respect the established rules" (Dreikurs and Grey 1968, pp. 71–72). Apart from the remarkable conservatism of Dreikurs's world view—more about which in the next chapter—there is not much reason to think that the distinction here will mean much to the average student. The teacher is the representative of the social order, the person who imposes a consequence for failing to respect the established rule. It is difficult to imagine that anyone will feel less put off by being made to undergo something unpleasant just because the teacher's goal has broader social ramifications.

The second set of criteria for defining logical consequences concerns their lack of harshness. The person who invokes them should be friendly and avoid scolding or judging (Dreikurs and Grey 1968, pp. 74, 77, 128); she should act in a "respectful" fashion and make sure the consequence itself is "reasonable" (Nelsen 1987, p. 73; also see Albert 1989, p. 79). Thus, if a student tips his chair back, it is supposedly a logical consequence for him to be forced to stand for the rest of the period (Albert 1989, p. 78).[6] Is this more reasonable than making him stand for, say, the rest of the week? Unquestionably. It is also more reasonable to paddle a child than to shoot him, but this does not offer much of an argument for paddling.

Likewise, is it more respectful if we announce in a matter-of-fact tone that the student will be forced to stand up, as opposed to screaming this at him? No doubt—but again, the nature of what we are doing remains pretty much the same. A punishment does not change its essential nature merely because it is less harsh or invoked in a softer tone of voice. Someone who wants to know whether a given intervention is punitive can find the answer not in a book on discipline but in the child's face.[7]

Imagine the face, for example, of the 2nd grade student who Dreikurs tells us is guilty of "talking out of turn, squirming, and so on" and who is ordered not only to leave the room but to spend time back in a kindergarten class. Dreikurs approves of this response so long as it does not seem "arbitrary": to ensure that it is a consequence rather than a punishment, the teacher need only strike the right tone by saying that she wonders whether he is "ready to continue in second grade" and suggesting that "it might be better for [him] to try and go back to kindergarten for a while" (Dreikurs and Grey 1968, pp. 143–44). If there is a difference between doing this to a child and engaging in old-fashioned punishment, it is at best a quantitative rather than a qualitative difference. What Dreikurs and his followers are selling is Punishment Lite.

# (IL)LOGICAL CONSEQUENCES

The third and most widely cited distinction between punishments and logical consequences is that the latter are related to what the child did wrong; there must be some connection between the child's action and the adult's reaction. By definition, a "consequence" fits the crime (Dreikurs and Grey 1968, pp. 73–74; Nelsen 1987, p. 73). This is really the linchpin of Dreikurs's system because of his core belief that "children retaliate [when they are punished] because they see no relationship between the punishment and the crime" (Dreikurs et al. 1982, p. 117). If this premise is wrong, then the whole house of cards—the distinction between consequences and punishments, and the rationale for the former—comes crashing down.

I believe it is wrong. To contrive some sort of conceptual link between the punishment and the crime may be satisfying to the adult, but in most cases it probably makes very little difference to the child. The child's (understandable) anger and desire to retaliate come from the fact that someone is deliberately making her suffer. That person is relying on power, forcing her to do something she doesn't want to do or preventing her from doing something she likes. The issue here is not the specific features of the coercive action so much as the coercion itself: "You didn't do what I wanted, so now I'm going to make something unpleasant happen to you." This power play invariably enrages the person who is being discomfited, in part because she is forced to confront her helplessness to do anything about it. We would not expect her anger to vanish just because of modest modifications in the implementation.

Now consider the following examples of "logical consequences" commended to us by Dreikurs and some of the New Discipline practitioners, and ask whether they would not meet any reasonable definition of punishment:

- If a child leaves his toys lying around at home, his mother is advised to hide them and, when asked, lie to the child by saying, "I'm sorry. I put them somewhere, but I don't remember right now." Dreikurs continues:

> Eventually, of course, the mother "finds" the toys, but not until the child had experienced the discomfort of being without some of his favorite playthings for a period of time. In another method—though not for the fainthearted—the parent "accidentally" steps on one of the child's favorite toys which has been left around (Dreikurs and Grey 1968, p. 96).

- Instead of sitting quietly, two 1st graders are using their hands to rehearse a dance they will be performing later. The teacher makes them come to the front of the room and tells them they must demonstrate the dance to the rest of the class. "Though the children were obviously embarrassed, it was a result of their own action and not a result of any arbitrary judgment by the teacher," we are told (Dreikurs and Grey 1968, pp. 142–143).
- A kindergarten girl who has bitten other children is required to wear a sign that reads "I bite people." This consequence, we are told, "shows ingenuity . . . and also courage" (Dreikurs and Grey 1968, p. 169).
- If a student makes a spitball, the teacher should force him to make 500 more spitballs so that his throat becomes "increasingly parched" (Albert 1989, p. 34).
- For various infractions, students are to be prevented from going to the library or from eating lunch in the cafeteria, told to sit in the principal's area, forced to miss a class field trip, or required to write an essay on how they "intend to stop breaking this rule" (Curwin and Mendler 1988, pp. 72, 81).
- If students have been noisy, the teacher should give an unannounced test with "the most difficult questions she can think of.

When the papers are returned, there should be as many low marks as are possible to give, though the results are not placed in the grade book" (Dreikurs and Grey 1968, p. 135).

- Children who do not comply with the teacher's wishes are isolated in a time-out area so they will "experience a few uncomfortable moments." More such moments are added for "repeat offenders" (Albert 1989, p. 77). However, the place where children are forced to sit by themselves can be made less punitive by calling it "the 'happy bench'" (Nelsen, Lott, and Glenn 1993, p. 124).

- "Each student who violates a rule [must] write his own name on the blackboard"—or, in another approach, must have his name written there by an elected class "sheriff" who is "responsible for keeping the behavioral records" (Curwin and Mendler 1988, p. 76).

- If a student has been disturbing the class, the teacher should "discuss the situation with the class" to "evoke group pressure" that will make him change his behavior—or alternatively, wait for a peaceful moment and then facetiously say to the student, in front of everyone, "You've been quiet for some time, wouldn't you like to say something?" (Dreikurs et al. 1982, p. 124, 132).[8]

These are only a few examles of the scores of suggestions offered by the New Discipline theorists; still others appear in books intended for parents. Even though many, if not all, would seem to be indistinguishable from punishments—and in some cases, rather cruel ones—we are reassured that we have done nothing more in each instance than to impose a logical consequence. In essence, the New Disciplines give us permision to "punish with impunity," in Marilyn Watson's apt phrase; they relieve us of a bad conscience and of the need to think about *real* alternatives to the paradigm of control.

Take another look at the case against punishing people (pp. 24–30): The punisher is only controlling the behavior—or trying to do so—rather than influencing the person who behaves. Temporary compliance will be purchased at the cost of making the student even angrier, and therefore making the problem worse in the long run. The relationship between the punisher and the punished is ruptured.

Attention is focused on avoiding the punishment, not on the action—and on how one is personally affected, not on the way others feel or what is the right thing to do.

Every one of these arguments applies to the use of so-called logical consequences. Consider the last point. The Discipline with Dignity program says we should be concerned with "developing an internal orientation" in students by asking them, "What do you think will happen if you do this [bad thing] again?" (Curwin and Mendler 1991, Part 2). In practice, that usually means "What do you think will happen *to you?*" The video for this program shows us successful applications of this question, in which students predict that they will get in trouble. The likely result of this strategy, however, is less an internal locus of control (as contrasted with being at the mercy of unpredictable forces) than a focus on self (rather than on others).

Do logical consequences "work"? One is naturally suspicious of unfalsifiable claims of success, such as this one: "Truly appropriate consequences will have a beneficial effect on students whether they let on or not" (Albert 1989, p. 82). But what Dreikurs observes about punishment can just as well be said of consequences: "the fact that the results were good does not make it a correct procedure" (Dreikurs and Grey 1968, pp. 164–165). Leaving a small child to cry himself to sleep can force him to learn how to console himself, but the emotional cost may be high. Likewise, even if a consequence did succeed in eliminating a misbehavior—which is by no means a likely outcome—we may have reason to doubt its wisdom.

## MORE OF THE SAME

Apart from the suggestions labeled as logical consequences, the New Disciplines offer a variety of other techniques for dealing with students who don't act the way we want. Once again, they bear a striking similarity to old-fashioned punishment. It's not surprising, for example, that someone who cheerfully tells us to become more "authoritarian" would recommend that when a student objects to something we say, we should just keep repeating our original "request . . . like a broken record" (McDaniel 1982, p. 247). But it may be surprising that a program called Cooperative Discipline, which claims to support a democratic, self-esteem-enhancing classroom, would offer exactly the same advice (Albert 1989, p. 75; also see Cline and Fay 1990, p. 83).

Of course, to say the same thing to (or at) a student over and over is to ignore what the student has to say. That advice is consistent with Dreikurs's suggestion that we should make a point of paying no attention to any student who does something "negative" (Dreikurs et al. 1982, pp. 34–37). And in case that doesn't work, we should play tit for tat: If a student has interrupted you, just wait until the next time *he* starts to answer a question and then cut him off abruptly and talk to someone else (Dreikurs and Grey 1968, pp. 148–149). One may be struck by how childish these responses are, or perhaps how likely they are to backfire in light of how they make students feel. But most of all, one is struck by how little they differ from the traditional punitive model.

The same may be said of an old standby used on young children: time out. This term originally was short for "time out from positive reinforcement," a practice developed to suppress certain behaviors in laboratory animals. Quite frankly, that fact alone gave me pause when I began to think about the topic, but before passing judgment I wanted to hear the opinions of educators whose work I already respected—particularly those with considerable experience in early childhood education.

The consensus seemed to be that sending someone away and forcing him to sit by himself does nothing to resolve whatever the problem was. It "cannot give a child new standards of behavior, insight into how one's actions affect others, or strategies for coping with an uncomfortable or painful situation," as Lilian Katz (1985, p. 3) has observed. The adult is not asking, "Why have you . . . ?" or even saying, "Here's why you might . . . " She is simply telling the child, "Do it my way or leave."

Yes, it's true that exiling a disruptive child can make everyone else feel better, at least for a while. But this means that time out acts as "a wedge that pushes persons into opposite directions. Some are feeling relieved at the same time that another person is feeling oppressed" (Lovett 1985, p. 16).

Adele Faber and Elaine Mazlish (1995, pp. 115–116), who have adapted some of their sensible parenting strategies for classroom use, ask us to put ourselves in the place of a child who is forcibly isolated: "As an adult you can imagine how resentful and humiliated you would feel if someone forced you into isolation for something you said or did." For a child, however, it is even worse, since she may come to believe "that there is something so wrong with her that she has to be removed from society." And Vivian Paley (1992, p. 95) adds that such feelings ultimately reverberate through the classroom:

> Thinking about unkindness always reminds me of the time-out chair. It made children sad and lonely to be removed from the group, which in turn made me feel inadequate and mean and— I became convinced—made everyone feel tentative and unsafe. These emotions show up in a variety of unwholesome ways depending on whether one is a teacher or child.

Let me be clear that there is nothing objectionable about having a safe, comfortable place where a child can go to calm down or just be alone for a few minutes. That's a terrific idea—so good, in fact, that adults can set a powerful example by taking some time by themselves to cool off when they feel angry. Children should be given this option, and when emotions are running high, they can be gently (and, if possible, privately) reminded that it exists. What Katz and Paley and the rest of us are talking about, though, is a situation where the child is *ordered* to leave the group, where, in the words of one fervent proponent, it is "a direction, *not* a negotiation" (Charney 1991, p. 95). In practice, that means it's a punishment—and for many children, a remarkably hurtful one.

However, for teachers who remain unconvinced that time out should be eliminated, I offer these suggestions for minimizing the damage. First, use time out only as a last resort, in extraordinary situations.[9] Second, do everything in your power to make it less punitive. The National Association for the Education of Young Children (1986) offers the following reasonable and important recommendations:

- Time out does not mean leaving the child alone, unless he or she wants to be. After the child has calmed down, the adult and child can talk about the child's feelings.

- Children should not be threatened with or afraid of a time out.

- Time out should not be humiliating. There should not be a predetermined time, chair, or place.

The last of these suggestions is particularly significant. If a teacher has established a "time-out chair"—or, worse, a formula for the number of minutes a child must spend in it—then the results are likely to be no better than we would expect with any other technique designed to make children unhappy.

# HEADS I WIN, TAILS YOU LOSE

Discussions of how to impose "logical consequences" and other punishments are often connected to the issue of choice. As we saw in Chapter 2, there is a relationship between insisting that students do, in fact, choose their behavior and making them suffer a punitive consequence for what they have "chosen."

But consider for a moment the question of whether students *should* be allowed to make choices. In the abstract, almost everyone says yes. Even Lee Canter (1988, p. 72), citing Dreikurs, agrees that "it is through choice that students learn about responsibility." But what exactly is meant by "choice"? That's the question we need to ask anyone who claims to endorse the concept. In practice, the word may be misleading; it may be used to describe situations in which students actually have very little opportunity to make meaningful decisions.

What is described as a choice may, in any of three distinct ways, actually be a pseudochoice.

**1. "Obey or suffer."** Canter (quoted in Hill 1990, p. 75) elaborates as follows on his idea of letting students make decisions: "The way you teach kids to be responsible is by telling them exactly what is expected of them and then giving them a choice" as to whether they comply.

Here we have a rather peculiar understanding of the word *responsible*, which looks suspiciously like a euphemism for "obedient" (see Appendix 2). But Canter's pronouncement also contains a sharply limited view of "choice," which amounts to either (a) doing "exactly what is expected" by the teacher or (b) facing the consequences.

Consistent with a pattern we have already noticed, the philosophy and techniques of Assertive Discipline are echoed in the New Disciplines, notwithstanding the claims of the latter to be substantially different. If a child is late returning from recess, for example, Dreikurs suggests that in the future we give her "a choice of returning with the others or standing by the teacher during recess until it is time to return to class" (Dreikurs et al. 1982, p. 123).

But children may not even get to recess in the first place if teachers have offered them the sort of choice described in Discipline with Dignity. A student who for any reason has not completed a task on (the teacher's) schedule is to be told, "You can do your assignment now or during recess" (Curwin and Mendler 1988, p. 15; also see Charney 1991, Collis and Dalton 1990). Remarkably, this is even commended to us as an illustration of letting students make decisions.

To begin with, notice that the options for the student have been gratuitously reduced to two—a practice that can sometimes be justified but ought not to be accepted without careful reflection.[10] On closer examination, though, these sorts of examples do not present children with a real choice at all. Typically no child wants to miss recess. The teacher is really saying, "Finish your work now or I'm going to take away something you like"—or, in generic terms, "Do what I tell you or I'm going to punish you."

Wrapping this threat in the language of choice allows the teacher to camouflage a conventional use of coercion by pretending to offer the student a chance to decide—or, in the sanitized language preferred by one proponent of this technique, the teacher is "using choices . . . to elicit or motivate desired behaviors" (Bluestein 1988, p. 149). The fact that these behaviors are desired—indeed, required—by someone else means that the putative chooser doesn't really have much choice at all. "As soon as we say 'Either you do this for me or I'll do that to you,' the child will feel trapped and hostile" (Faber and Mazlish 1995, p. 90).

**2. "You punished yourself."** In a variation of this gambit that is a hallmark of Assertive Discipline, students are punished after disobeying the teacher's command, but the punishment is presented as something they asked for: "If they choose to behave in an inappropriate manner" as determined unilaterally by the teacher, "they will also choose to accept the negative consequences of that choice" (Canter and Canter 1992, p. 169). Thus: "You have chosen to sit by yourself at the table" (p. 81); "you will choose to have your parents called" (p. 194); and so on.

Once again, the New Disciplines follow in lockstep. In Discipline with Dignity, we are encouraged to tell students who break the rules that they have "chosen to go home for the rest of the day" (Curwin and Mendler 1988, p. 15) or have "chosen five minutes in Siberia (time-out area)" (p. 107). In Cooperative Discipline, a child is likewise told that she has "chosen to go to [time-out in] Mr. Jordan's room" (Albert 1989, p. 77). And in a book called *Teaching Children to Care*, we find the same thing: "I see you are choosing to go to your time-out place" (Charney 1991, p. 114).[11]

Again, the appeal of this tactic is no mystery: it seems to relieve the teacher of responsibility for what he is about to do to the child. (Apparently, students not only always choose their own behavior, but also choose the teacher's response! Teachers would seem to be exempt from the axiom that people are responsible for their own choices.)

Even in cases where we really can state unconditionally that a child has "chosen" to do something bad—notwithstanding the concerns about such sweeping statements raised in Chapter 2—the child certainly does not choose to be punished for it. The teacher does that to him. In short, this is a fundamentally dishonest, not to mention manipulative, attribution. To the injury of punishment is added the insult of a kind of mind game whereby reality is redefined and children are told, in effect, that they wanted to have something bad happen to them (see Crockenberg 1982, pp. 65–70).

"You've chosen a time out" is a lie: a truthful teacher would have to say, "I've chosen to isolate you."

**3. "Choose . . . and Suffer."** In yet another version of pseudochoice, children are allowed or even encouraged to make certain decisions specifically so they will suffer from their own poor judgment. This technique falls under the rubric of what Dreikurs called natural (as distinct from logical) consequences, which he defined somewhat circularly as "the natural results of ill-advised acts" (Dreikurs and Grey 1968, p. 63).

Of course, there is a kernel of truth here: many times, we do learn from the unpleasant results that follow from poor choices. If I leave my books too close to the edge of the desk, they may fall over; if I stay up late, I'm probably going to be tired in the morning. However, letting a child experience the "natural consequences" of her action may not be particularly constructive, depending on her age, the nature of the action, and other factors. Many people like to point out, for example, that a child who constantly insults her peers will soon have few friends as a result. But to conclude that this will "teach" her to be a nicer person overlooks basic human psychology—specifically, the reciprocal relation between perceptions and behaviors, and the way they can spiral out of control. The fact that others steer clear of this child may simply cement her disagreeable image of them—or of herself.

Similarly, an aggressive child may eventually get his teeth knocked out by someone bigger than he is, but this will likely teach him the importance of making sure that he wins the next fight, not the futility (much less the immorality) of fighting. Lilian Katz (1984, p. 9) has observed that "the school of hard knocks, although powerful, is likely to provide the wrong lessons to children"—and the same could be said about many natural consequences.

In a program called Discipline with Love and Logic, children aren't merely allowed to live with the results of their actions; they are "forced to make . . . decisions" so that they will come to regret the bad ones (Cline and Fay 1990, p. 48). As a result, "children don't get angry at us; they get angry at themselves" (p. 78; also see Dreikurs et al. 1982, p. 118). The authors are quite clear about the intent: "We want our kids to *hurt from the inside out*" (Cline and Fay 1990, p. 91; emphasis in original). The sample dialogues offered in this manual suggest a smug satisfaction on the part of the adult who watches as children "learn" (read: suffer) from their own mistakes.

The salient questions here are these: What message do adults send when they deliberately allow something unpleasant to happen to a child even though they could have intervened? What conclusions does the child draw about how much the adult cares about him, or whether he is worth caring about, or how he should come to regard other people in general? Incredibly, the authors of Discipline with Love and Logic talk about the importance of empathy, even though precisely the opposite of empathic concern would seem to be communicated to a child by an adult following their prescription.

In conventional punishment, a child is at least left with a sense of self intact and the capacity to stand in opposition to the punisher. Not so with this insidious strategy, which tries to turn the child against herself. Any doubt about the lack of respect for children demonstrated by this approach is erased when the authors give us leave to ignore any objections that children may make to something we have done to them: "Once you encounter resistance, you'll know [the technique is] working" (p. 103).

A caring adult wants to help children learn to make responsible decisions about the things that matter to them—and to help them see the results of those decisions. That, however, is very different from what has become of the concept of choice in the New Discipline programs. Here, "consequences" are neither logical nor natural.

\* \* \*

This chapter should not be taken to imply that there is nothing at all to recommend any of the New Discipline programs—or that they are interchangeable with each other, or just as coercive as Assertive Discipline. For example, there is no mistaking the latter for most of

*Positive Discipline in the Classroom* (Nelsen et al. 1993), whose central concern is to let students participate in decision making through the vehicle of class meetings. The other programs, too, talk about phrasing requests respectfully, avoiding interventions that amount to public humiliations, and so on. Credit should be given for these and comparable features that are more humane than other approaches to classroom management.

But a careful reading of the New Disciplines compels the unhappy conclusion that, on balance, most of them are remarkably similar to the old-school approach in their methods—and, as we are about to see, their goals. These programs are merely packaged in such a way as to appeal to educators who are uncomfortable with the idea of using bribes and threats. The truth is what it has always been: a ruse is a ruse is a ruse.

∞

# HOW NOT TO GET CONTROL OF THE CLASSROOM

Moral autonomy appears when the mind regards as necessary an ideal that is independent of all external pressure.

—JEAN PIAGET, *THE MORAL JUDGMENT OF THE CHILD*

A seemingly benign and kindly form of control, to bend rather than break a child's will . . . [is] unlikely to create a genuine sense of autonomy in the child, or a sense of choice and responsibility.

—PHILIP GREVEN, *SPARE THE CHILD*

∞

## EFFECTIVE . . . BUT AT WHAT?

The preceding two chapters argued, first, that it doesn't make much sense to punish or reward students, and second, that discipline programs typically rely on punishing and rewarding students (whether or not these words are used). Now it is time to dig beneath the *methods* of discipline and take a look at the underlying *goals*. Simply criticizing what is going on in classrooms, or proposing new techniques, seems to beg the question—and the question is: What are we trying to do here?

This issue is rarely addressed explicitly by people who conduct research on classroom management programs. However, the way their studies measure the "effectiveness" of these programs suggests a distinct set of assumptions about what teachers ought to be doing. Consider one of the classic publications in the field, an early attempt to be scientific about discipline. After videotaping several dozen primary grade classrooms, Jacob Kounin (1970) identified a few key teacher variables as keys to success. Of these, the one that has been most widely cited was rather cutely called "withitness." This term meant the teacher not only was attentive to what students were doing, but let them know she knew what was going on; she developed a reputation for having, as it were, eyes in the back of her head. Such teachers were shown to be more effective than their withoutit colleagues.

But what does it mean in this context to be "effective"? To Kounin, it meant getting "conformity and obedience" (p. 65); it meant students didn't do whatever was defined as "deviant" and kept busy at "the assigned work" (p. 77). Now, if a good classroom is one where students simply do what they're told, we shouldn't be surprised that a teacher is more likely to have such a classroom when students are aware that she can quickly spot noncompliance. After all, if a good society was defined as one where citizens obey any and every governmental decree, then scholars might be able to adduce scientific evidence that a good leader is one who resembles Orwell's Big Brother.

In fact, researchers since Kounin have found that classroom management was most effective "when long periods of student talk (recitations) were avoided. In other words, the teacher retained control over pacing." For that matter, the effective teachers retained control over just about everything, closely directing and monitoring students and providing tasks that were "very highly structured" (Emmer and Evertson 1981, pp. 345, 343). Again, these results are perfectly logical if we accept the premises; the techniques follow naturally from the objective. The objective is not to promote depth of understanding, or continuing motivation to learn, or concern for others. It is to maximize time on task and obedience to authority.

The point here is not to criticize how research is conducted; it is to ask what the whole enterprise of "classroom management" is about. Contrary to claims often made in its behalf, it does not merely signify a set of procedures that enable educators to more effectively reach any goals they may happen to have. The very idea of classroom management, far from being neutral, enfolds within it certain goals. And these goals may well be seen as highly problematic.

## "SIT DOWN AND SHUT UP"

If researchers usually fail to address such issues head on, at least many of the people who design and sell discipline plans are quite clear about their objectives. In certain manuals written for parents, the goal may even appear right on the cover. For example, a book called *Magic 1-2-3* (Phelan 1995) carries the subtitle "Training Your Children to Do What *You* Want" (emphasis in original). Both the first word, which is deliberately intended to evoke the control of animal behavior,[1] and the italicized word, which suggests that children's own needs and desires don't matter, leave no doubt about the point of the program.

Even when classroom management guides don't talk about "training" students, it isn't unusual to find a subtitle or chapter title such as "Guidelines for Maintaining Control." Even more commonly, articles about discipline in education magazines take for granted that our chief concern should be to get students to comply with our wishes. We are advised to tell children in no uncertain terms how we expect them to behave, to impose "limits" as we see fit, and to announce what will happen to anyone who disobeys. In short, the prescription is *dictate, control,* and *threaten.* An effective teacher by definition is one who manages to get compliance with minimal effort and who succeeds in forcing rebellious children to back down (e.g., Jones 1979).

Assertive Discipline, the best-known of these systems for making the trains run on time in the classroom, was introduced in the mid-1970s. (For a tongue-in-cheek guide to some key terms in this program, see Appendix 2.) The latest edition of the Assertive Discipline manual contains a bit of perfunctory talk about helping students to develop "responsibility" and "self-esteem," but even the most cursory exposure to the program makes it clear that the overriding goal is to get students to do whatever they are told without question. Teachers are encouraged to remove anyone who misbehaves because this "gives you back the control of the classroom" (Canter and Canter 1992, p. 87). That the teacher *ought* to have unilateral control is not a proposition to be defended; it is a premise, a first principle. And if students balk at the demand for obedience—or at anything else—it doesn't matter. All that counts, as Canter states with remarkable candor, is that they capitulate:

> Whenever possible, simply ignore the covert hostility of a student. By ignoring the behavior you will diffuse [sic] the situation. Remember, what you really want is for the student to comply with your request. Whether or not the student does it in an angry manner is not the issue. The student is still complying with your expectations (Canter and Canter 1992, p. 180).

Even when judged by the narrow criterion of getting children to conform, the evidence suggests that Assertive Discipline is not terribly effective. When various approaches to classroom management are examined empirically, some studies typically show "positive" effects while others show no effects. It is rare to discover that a program has negative effects, but they have turned up in some studies of Assertive Discipline. Overall, most of the published research shows the technique to be detrimental or, at best, to have no meaningful effect at all (Emmer and Aussiker 1990; Render, Padilla, and Krank 1989).

Still, one of the chief selling points of a program like Assertive Discipline is, in the words of one teacher, that "it's easy to use. It's all spelled out for you" (Hill 1990, p. 75). Without a packaged system, Canter warns, the teacher would be "forced to constantly make choices about how to react to student behavior" (Canter and Canter 1992, p. 46). In other words, the teacher might have to think for herself or bring students into the process of solving problems. The late John Nicholls spent a year watching a 2nd grade teacher struggle to implement Assertive Discipline and observed that it "stifled her wit and cut her off from the children she communicates with so well" (Nicholls and Hazzard 1993, p. 187). Indeed, teachers who have abandoned the program in favor of a noncoercive model of teaching sometimes say they would quit the profession before using Assertive Discipline again.

A few years ago, a writer asked me whether I thought this program would be around long enough to warrant her taking the time to criticize it in a book she was writing on another topic. As I pondered her question, I found my reactions shifting. My first thought was: "By all means! Hundreds of thousands of teachers[2] have been exposed to this set of techniques, and many have never been helped to reflect on how destructive it really is."

Then I reconsidered. It's too easy, I realized, to blame a single person or program for what is disturbing about American schools. Canter has often pointed out that "there is nothing new about Assertive Discipline," that it is "simply a systematization" of common behavior management strategies (Canter 1989, p. 631)—and he is absolutely right. If this program disappeared from the face of the earth tomorrow, another collection of bribes and threats would take its place. It is really these generic techniques that need to be uprooted.

Only gradually did I realize that even this was not the last word. Rewards and punishments are instruments for controlling people, and the real problem, I came to see, is the belief that the teacher should be in control of the classroom, that the principal objective— and sometimes the objective of the principal—is just to get students to comply. In this chapter, and implicitly through the remainder of the book, I will try to show why this common assumption is so troubling and what the alternative looks like. Before doing so, however, let us take a quick look at the New Disciplines to see whether their objectives are any different.

## "BE SEATED AND REFRAIN FROM TALKING"

If you ask the purveyors of the New Disciplines what they are trying to accomplish, you will often hear broad, laudable goals concerning children's psychological development. There are even occasional denunciations of mindless conformity: we are told that "obedience, even when it 'works,' is not . . . defensible" (Curwin and Mendler 1988, pp. 23–24) and that "the more voice and choice students have, the more cooperative and responsible they'll act and feel" (Albert 1989, p. 19).

What really counts, however, is what goes on in a classroom where such a program is in operation. What would be inferred by a visitor who had never read the rhetoric? What philosophy is implied by the specific practical recommendations? The answer, I have reluctantly concluded, is that the New Disciplines are just as much about getting compliance as is the more traditional approach. The overriding goal is to get students to do "what they are supposed to be doing" (Curwin and Mendler 1991), to "learn what's acceptable [to the teacher] and what's not" (Albert 1989, p. 67).

Indeed, we are tipped off from the start by the fact that presentations on these programs often begin with a nostalgic nod to the good old days when students did what the teacher asked without questioning. More significantly, these systems accept—also without questioning—that it is desirable, if not necessary, for teachers to be in control of their classrooms. The only issues are how benevolent that controller will be and how respectfully she will get and maintain the control. This imperative is hard to miss in many of the quotations from New Discipline books and videos that I have already cited.

For Rudolf Dreikurs, getting students to do what the teacher tells them is only a means to an end. His ultimate objective seems to be preserving the status quo in the broadest sense. On the very first page of his major tract on logical consequences (written in the 1960s), Dreikurs offers a bitter condemnation of social unrest that lumps together protest marches and juvenile delinquency (Dreikurs and Grey 1968, p. 3). He goes on to indignantly denounce how "parents are called upon to justify their actions in ways which were not expected of them in the past" (p. 4) and how "today children are free to do as they please" (pp. 20–21). Sprinkled throughout the book are remarks about the need "to keep things moving smoothly" (p. 153) and the importance of "respect for order" (p. 125) and getting children to "learn to respect the established rules" (p. 72).

In Dreikurs's other books—and those of the authors influenced by him—there is much talk about "democracy" and the importance of replacing crude coercion with modern methods such as mutual respect and dialogue. At first, it isn't easy to explain how these ideas could exist side by side with a list of "consequences" that seem almost sadistic. Likewise, one struggles to understand how a section of one of his books entitled "Democratic Practices" could contain such suggestions as using a class meeting to drive "a wedge between the participants, splitting them up [so as] to weaken their power. The moment the teacher wins one or more of the students, it fortifies her position" (Dreikurs et al. 1982, p. 237).

But the apparent contradiction dissolves once we recognize the very specific, and rather peculiar, meaning Dreikurs gives to democracy. In a pivotal sentence, he declares: *"It is autocratic to force, but democratic to induce compliance"* (Dreikurs et al. 1982, p. 67; emphasis added). And later: "Children should be stimulated to want to conform" (pp. 85–86). Given this perspective, it makes sense that discussion sessions would be used strategically by teachers to "induce compliance." Dreikurs is decidedly not talking about offering students a genuine opportunity to participate in decision making.

Some discipline practitioners shy away from explicit talk of compliance. Their language is lovelier and their techniques are trendier, but ultimately their systems are woven from the same cloth. For someone interested in goals, it makes little difference whether one resorts to nods and smiles rather than scowls and shouts, whether one prefers class meetings, positive reinforcement, or old-fashioned punishment. What counts is that the teacher has never given up any real control. What matters is that the goal is not learning: it is obedience.

# THE PROBLEM WITH COMPLIANCE

Like a few other people I know who conduct workshops, I like to start a session by asking participants to think about the following question: "What are your long-term goals for the students you work with? What would you like them to be—to be like—long after

60

they've left you?" After a moment, I ask what words or phrases have come to mind, and I write on a flip chart each answer that is volunteered. Then I ask the group to reflect on the list as a whole and see if any generalizations suggest themselves.

The document that emerges almost always describes a certain kind of person rather than just a certain kind of learner. Psychological and social characteristics (for example, "caring," "happy," and "responsible") predominate over those relating to intellect. Moreover, someone invariably notices that even those goals that do pertain to intellectual development have been conceived broadly ("curious," "creative," "lifelong learners") rather than in terms of specific academic content. In all the times I have done this activity in different parts of the country, no educator—or parent, for that matter—has ever said that his or her long-term goal for students is for them to know how to solve an equation with two variables, or remember the names of the explorers of the New World.

This simple exercise, which I recommend for virtually any staff development session or faculty meeting, is so useful because it is so unsettling. It is unsettling because it exposes a yawning chasm between what we want and what we are doing, between how we would like students to turn out and how our classrooms and schools actually work. We want children to continue reading and thinking after school has ended, yet we focus their attention on grades, which have been shown to reduce interest in learning (Kohn 1993a, 1994). We want them to be critical thinkers, yet we feed them predigested facts and discrete skills—partly because of pressure from various constituencies to pump up standardized test scores. We act as though our goal is short-term retention of right answers rather than genuine understanding.

These points have been made before. But now consider the non-academic goals, which seem to be at least as important to educators and parents. Just as no one offers specific academic content as a long-term objective, so no one says, "I want my kids to obey authority without question, to be compliant and docile."

Now maybe the people who attend my workshops are strikingly unrepresentative of American educators, or maybe those who do show up are just too embarrassed to admit that they are hoping to produce compliant people. You will have to judge for yourself, based on your own goals and those of your colleagues, how typical and candid are the responses I'm reporting here. But if compliance is, in fact, not what most of us are looking for in the long run, then we may be faced with the same basic conflict: our ultimate objectives for kids versus our short-term goals (control of the classroom) and methods (coercion, consequences, rewards). Something has got to give.

What I've been arguing, over the course of several chapters, is that desirable outcomes are harder to achieve if we rely on bribes and threats. Even when children are "successfully" rewarded or threatened into compliance, they will likely feel no commitment to what they are doing, no deep understanding of the act and its rationale, no sense of themselves as the kind of people who would *want* to act this way in the future. Remember: they have been led to concentrate on the consequences of their actions to themselves, and someone with this frame of reference bears little resemblance to the kind of person we dream of seeing our students become.

But now we are ready to move beyond a critique of punishment and rewards. The next step is to recognize that trying to keep control of the classroom and get compliance, as virtually every discipline program assures us we must, is inimical to our ultimate objectives. What we have to face is that *the more we "manage" students' behavior and try to make them do what we say, the more difficult it is for them to become morally sophisticated people who think for themselves and care about others.*

This proposition immediately leads some people to ask: Aren't there times when we simply need students to do what we tell them? To answer this question thoughtfully, we should begin by observing that the number of those occasions seems to vary quite a bit from one teacher to the next. This fact suggests that the "need" for compliance is less a function of some objective feature of the situation than of the teacher's personality and background—or of the pressures brought to bear by others (for example, to have one's classroom "under control"). Thus, we ought to examine our preferences rather than taking them for granted. If I discover that I need students to be more compliant than you do, I should not feel entitled to use a coercive discipline program; rather, I should examine the source of my demand for compliance.*

So does this mean that anything goes? Does it mean that students don't have to comply with our preference for them to study, that they can ignore their assignments, shout obscenities, or create havoc? This sort of scenario is frequently invoked as a way of fending off challenges to the way things have always been done. But it misses the point. The question isn't whether it's OK for students to act in those ways. Rather, the question is whether they are likely to do so in the absence of a teacher-controlled, compliance-oriented classroom.

If we reject an unduly pessimistic view of children's basic motives, if we recognize that the quality of the curriculum has a lot to do with students' enthusiasm (or its absence), then we will be less likely to revert to the simplistic opposition of control versus chaos, in which teachers think they "must choose between putting up with behavior problems and being the big boss and stamping them out" (Nicholls and Hazzard 1993, p. 56). False dichotomies like this one are popular in part because they make choosing easy: clearly we don't want chaos, therefore there's only one road to take. But in the kind of classroom I will be describing, the teacher works with students to create a democratic community. He is much less concerned with his own status as the authority figure, and much less enamored of a goal like "inducing compliance."

Paradoxically, students in such classrooms are more likely to comply when it is truly necessary for them to do so—and, yes, of course, there will be such times. In certain situations, any teacher will need students just to do what she says, period. But students are more apt to trust her and go along if blind obedience is the exception rather than the rule in her classroom—which is to say, if she makes a habit of trusting *them* and has earned their respect. I am talking about a teacher who doesn't compel kids to learn or care *because she said so,* but instead helps them to experience the value of learning and caring.

---

* See the discussion in Chapter 2 about focusing on the child who doesn't do what he's told as opposed to reconsidering what he has been told to do.

But hold on. Even if our ultimate goal is for students to do the right thing for the right reason, don't we have to start out by demanding compliance? Doesn't the teacher need to have control of the classroom initially, as a prerequisite for achieving more ambitious and worthy ends?

Before answering that question, let's do a quick reality check. How often are these ends the real reason for taking control? We can search through countless articles and books on classroom management without finding any evidence that the writers are ultimately trying to empower children but just have a different way of getting there.* Indeed, the children themselves know full well that compliance remains the real point throughout the school year. When 4th graders in a variety of classrooms, representing a range of teaching styles and socioeconomic backgrounds, were surveyed about what their teachers most wanted them to do, they didn't say, "Ask thoughtful questions" or "Make responsible decisions" or "Help others." They said: "Be quiet, don't fool around, and get our work done on time" (LeCompte 1978, p. 30). Similarly, in interviews with 2nd and 6th graders that probed their beliefs about what it means to "behave well," the most common single answer had to do with keeping quiet (Blumenfeld, Pintrich, and Hamilton 1986).

But let's say a teacher really did want to help students take responsibility for themselves, to be capable decision makers and self-directed learners. Would she nevertheless have to start the year by securing control of the classroom in order to reach these goals? Absolutely not. In fact, to do so would make it far more difficult to be successful later on.

---

*Whether most educators really see control of the classroom as a necessary evil that facilitates *academic* learning is also open to debate. As Linda McNeil (1986, pp. 157–158) has observed, "many teachers . . . maintain discipline by the ways they present course content." To turn teaching into a transfer of disconnected facts and skills, for example, makes it easier to keep control. One traditionalist says that teachers should start the day with a "review drill" precisely because such an exercise "becomes a control mechanism" [McDaniel 1982, p. 247]. Curricular design, in other words, may actually be the means, with control being the end—thus turning the conventional wisdom on its head.

From the first day of school, a teacher chooses a style of leadership (ranging from autocratic to democratic) and sends a message about whose classroom it is (his or everyone's). It has often been observed that a teacher who seems indifferent and irrelevant to what the students are doing will have a hard time playing a more active role later on. Fair enough. But it is just as true that a teacher whose style is controlling, whose chief goal is to get obedience, who unilaterally decides on the "expectations" for what will happen in the room and imposes these on students, will not find it easy to transform that environment.

You may be familiar with the hoary educational adage that teachers should not smile until Christmas (or even Easter)—that is, that they should be severe and controlling for months and only then relent a bit, displaying a bit of kindness and revealing themselves to be actual human beings. I don't know who came up with that appalling saying, but I can only hope that he or she is no longer in a position to do harm to children. It is difficult to imagine an approach more out of step with everything we know about child development and learning. Even construed narrowly, that advice makes no sense: the available research "clearly demonstrates that nice teachers are highly effective . . . [and refutes] the myth that students learn more from cold, stern, distant teachers" (Andersen and Andersen 1987, pp. 57–58)—except, of course, that they may learn to be cold, stern, and distant themselves.

I have to believe that few educators would deliberately refrain from smiling. But quite a number subscribe—indeed, are trained to subscribe—to the fundamentally similar belief that control must come first. Some may even use smiles to gain that control. My contention is that a different set of goals and practices makes sense from the very beginning.

## MAKING MORAL MEANING

One way to talk about compliance is to say that the goal is to get children to learn the "appropriate" behavior, as designated by someone else. This approach is strikingly similar to the traditional model of academic instruction, where information or skills are transmitted to students so they will be able to produce correct answers on demand. For anyone who understands the limits of a "right answer" approach to learning, it can be illuminating to see that classroom management is basically about eliciting the "right behavior." This analogy also may help us to think about what we could be accomplishing instead.

The "constructivist" model of learning challenges the central metaphors that so often drive instruction. Children, like adults, are not passive receptacles into which knowledge is poured. They are not clay to be molded, or computers to be programmed, or animals to be trained. Rather, they are active meaning makers, testing out theories and trying to make sense of themselves and the world around them. Learning comes from discovering surprising things— perhaps from grappling with a peer's different perspective—and feeling the need to reformulate one's own approach. It entails playing with words and numbers and ideas, coming to understand these things from the inside out and making them one's own. Skills are acquired in the course of arriving at that deep and personal understanding, and in the context of seeking answers to one's own questions.

When children are instead required to accept or memorize a ready-made truth, they do not really "learn" in any meaningful sense of the word. This is what we witness when students have to do problem sets in math, multiplying rows of naked numbers; or make their way through worksheets until they can identify vowels or verbs; or slog through textbook lessons about scientific laws or historical events. This may be the way to prepare children to take standardized tests (though it doesn't appear very successful); it is not the way to help them become learners. "Teachers everywhere lament how quickly students forget" what they've learned, but the students "haven't forgotten; they never learned that which we assumed they had" (Brooks and Brooks 1993, pp. 39–40). At best, they learned how to spit out someone else's right answers.

Exactly the same is true if those right answers concern how one is supposed to *act*. I can get a child to recite "We should keep our hands and feet to ourselves" by repeating it enough times or by posting it on the wall, just as I can get her to recite "To divide by a fraction, turn it upside down and multiply." I can get a child to stop slugging someone (at least in my presence) by threatening to punish him if he continues, just as I can get him to pick out the topic sentence of a paragraph. But the first examples in each pair don't suggest someone who is developing socially or morally, any more than the latter examples suggest someone who is developing intellectually.

The only way to help students become ethical people, as opposed to people who merely do what they are told, is to have them construct moral meaning. It is to help them figure out—for themselves and with each other—how one ought to act. That's why dropping the tools of traditional discipline, like rewards and consequences, is only the beginning. It's even more crucial that we overcome a preoccupation with getting compliance and instead bring students in on the process of devising and justifying ethical principles.

This approach can be observed in classrooms scattered here and there across the country, and it is reflected in the work of the Child Development Project (which I describe in Chapter 7). It is also described in a pathbreaking book for early childhood educators[3] entitled *Moral Classrooms, Moral Children* by Rheta DeVries and Betty Zan (1994).

DeVries, along with Constance Kamii (1984, 1991; Kamii, Clark, and Dominick 1994), has her roots in a constructivist approach to math and science education for young children. But both of these researchers, drawing on the work of Jean Piaget (1965), also argue that children must actively invent (and reinvent) ethical meaning, just as they must construct mathematical meaning. In taking this position, they join the late Lawrence Kohlberg (e.g., Kohlberg and Mayer 1972; Power, Higgins, and Kohlberg 1989), who spent his career applying Piagetian notions of cognitive development to the moral realm—and other early childhood specialists such as Carolyn Edwards (1986) and Lilian Katz (1984)—in emphasizing that getting children to comply cannot be the teacher's primary goal.

Of course, merely *telling* teachers to stop focusing on compliance isn't any more likely to lead to real change than is merely telling children to act responsibly. But we can encourage teachers to think about their long-term goals and about whether their classrooms are really animated by these goals. Anyone can nod in agreement with such objectives as helping kids to develop an intrinsic commitment to good values, but does one's classroom reflect that concern? Or is the real point, day to day, simply to get kids to do what they're told?

We also have to identify particular assumptions and practices that accompany the quest for compliance—and to help others (and ourselves) think about them from a constructivist point of view. Two of those constellations of issues are addressed at length in the following chapters: first, maximizing the opportunity for students to make choices, to discover and learn for themselves; and second, creating a caring community in the classroom so that students have the opportunity to do these things *together*.

Even before addressing these broad issues, though, I'd like to look at three overlapping aspects of a constructivist approach that directly challenge conventional classroom management: moving beyond a focus on *behavior,* on *rules,* and on *ending conflict.*

## BEHAVIORS VS. PEOPLE

The developer of one New Discipline program has described its goal as getting students to "choose appropriate behaviors." That sounds at first like nothing more than plain common sense. But on reflection, there is reason to be concerned about each of those three words and the model that informs them.

The use of "choose," as I noted earlier, raises questions about the extent to which students are really just expected to do what someone else has decided, rather than having the chance to make any real choices. It's often a way of blaming students for things about which they had little to say. As for the modifier "appropriate," we might respond, "Appropriate to whom? And why?" To fudge those questions, as discipline programs tend to do, is to guarantee a system based on obedience.

But even to aim at getting certain "behaviors" from students is problematic. To focus on changing how a student *acts* virtually guarantees the use of carrots and sticks, which manipulate actions. Or, to put it the other way around, the techniques of applied behaviorism suggest a tacit reliance on behaviorist theory. Giving rewards (or "reinforcers") for compliance can be traced back to B.F. Skinner's view of all organisms, including us, as devoid of selves. We are nothing more than "repertoires of behaviors" that can, in turn, be completely explained in terms of things outside of us ("environmental contingencies").

You may not be sympathetic—or even familiar—with this odd, shrunken view of what it is to be human. But any time educators (or parents) frame the issue in terms of the need to change a child's behavior, they are unwittingly buying into a larger theory, one that excludes what many of us would argue are the things that really matter: the child's thoughts and feelings, needs and perspectives, motives and values—the things, in short, that result in certain behaviors. The behavior is only the surface phenomenon; what matters is the person who behaves . . . and *why* she does so.

Here are two students in two different classrooms, each of whom just gave half his lunch to someone else. The first student did so in the hope that the teacher would notice this and praise him: "Isn't that a nice thing to do! I'm so proud of you! I really appreciate your sharing like that!" The second student did so without knowing or caring whether the teacher saw him: he was simply concerned that the kid sitting next to him might go hungry.

The two behaviors are identical. What matters are the reasons and feelings that lie beneath. Discipline programs can (temporarily) change behavior, but they cannot help people to grow. The latter requires a very different orientation in the classroom: looking "through" a given action in order to understand the motives that gave rise to it as well as figuring out how to have some effect on those motives.

Consider, then, a specific contrast between two ways of responding to a child who shared his lunch. The teacher who is preoccupied with the behavior—and who seeks, in this case, to produce more of it—would probably resort to praise. A different approach, derived from Martin Hoffman's work on "inductive discipline" (Hoffman and Saltzstein 1967), would be to help the child attend to how his decision to share has affected someone else (in this case, the recipient of his food). "Boy, would you look at Jaime's face! He is one happy guy now that he has enough to eat, isn't he?"

The message of praise is: I approve of what you did, so you should do it again. It is a way of reinforcing the act.* "Look at Jaime's face!", on the other hand, is concerned with helping the sharer to experience the effects of sharing and to come to see himself as the kind of person who wants to make other people feel good—irrespective of verbal rewards.[4] Even when this particular response isn't used, the goal remains much deeper than buying a behavior; it is nothing less than assisting children in constructing an image of themselves as decent people.

## BEYOND RULES

Behaviorism lives on, not only in stickers and stars but in lists of concrete rules telling children exactly what they must, or must not, do. In Assertive Discipline, broader guidelines ("Treat each other kindly") are explicitly repudiated in favor of specific prescriptions ("Keep hands and feet to yourself") and proscriptions ("No profanity"): "The more observable a rule is, the easier it is for students to understand and comply with it" (Canter and Canter 1992, p. 51). Once again, Discipline with Dignity follows Canter's lead: "Rules work best when they are behavioral and written in black-and-white terms" (Curwin and Mendler 1988, p. 21).

Much is made of the need to spell out these rules (and the consequences that invariably accompany them) in advance, in order to provide "predictability." (Also, doing so may help to silence the inevitable complaints of unfairness in an environment defined by punitive consequences.) Thus, a teacher in the Discipline with Dignity video (Curwin and Mendler 1991) is brought on camera to announce with some satisfaction that her students are "aware, when they've broken a rule, what's going to happen, how it's going to happen, and when it's going to happen."

---

*Interestingly, despite the behavioral focus, this practice probably does make a deeper change in the child's way of looking at the world—for the worse. He is led to become concerned primarily with getting the adult's approval.

Unfortunately, the real message communicated in such a classroom is that it is not a community where troublesome behavior is a problem to be solved together; it is a place where the teacher says, "Do what I tell you, or here's *exactly* what I'll do to you." Just as a threat is no less a threat simply because it is uttered calmly, so a threat does not change its nature merely because it is spelled out ahead of time. If anything, the advance notice enhances its salience.[5]

An article entitled (without irony) "How to Be an Effective Authoritarian" offers the following as its first piece of practical advice: "Rules should be *specific*. . . . So that students do not have to define the real meaning of a rule, state it in specific, objective terms" (McDaniel 1982, p. 246). Notice that this prescription is more than behaviorism come to life; it is also, true to the essay's title, authoritarianism come to life. If the overriding objective is to get students to do whatever the teacher demands, it makes perfect sense to spell out specific rules that mandate specific behaviors. If, however, the goal is to help students grow into compassionate, principled people, then having students "define the real meaning" of rules is the best way— perhaps the only way—that a list of rules prepared by the teacher can help students become thoughtful decision makers. But such an arrangement can only do so much: it is far better to ask children to create the rules.

Some classroom management programs now suggest bringing students in on the rule-making process. But it's important to realize that this idea does not in itself reflect a constructivist perspective. For example, a program may allow, or even encourage, us to react with relief when a student comes up with the very rules that we had in mind: "What we have found is that the kids will either come up with the same rules [as the teacher's] or even tougher rules, but then they have ownership and you can label them 'We decided' instead of 'I decided'" (Nelsen et al. 1993, p. 140).

An adult with more ambitious objectives might well view such a neat correspondence with concern: students may be saying what they think the teacher wants to hear, or reciting what they memorized in previous years. No learning has taken place in such a transaction, nor has any moral or intellectual growth. The point may be, as it seems to be with Dreikurs, to foster the *appearance* of participation in order to secure compliance.

Some teachers (and consultants) have more on their minds than getting kids to obey: they genuinely want to create a classroom where students are respectful of one another. But they try to reach these objectives by drilling students in the right way to act (e.g., Charney 1991). Students have no opportunity to reflect on why it may be the right way, nor any chance to disagree. Their job is to say and do what they are told. The fact that you or I may be entirely sympathetic with *what* they are told—for example, the importance of respecting other people's feelings—shouldn't blind us to the limits of what can be achieved by merely telling people something. We ought to be concerned when even "very reasonable rules [are] . . imposed and enforced from above, with little opportunity for students to develop an understanding of or personal commitment to them" (Lewis 1995, p. 144). (A reliable earmark of this "imposed from above" approach is the use of public praise to reinforce certain behaviors.)

If students are to create rules, the teacher must be clear (first in her own mind, then with them) that the point is just that: to create. Student-generated rules that emerge from a deep and ongoing conversation are likely to be valuable not because of the rules themselves but because of the conversation that gave rise to them. *The process is the point.*

But let's go even further. From a constructivist perspective, the very idea of rules may be troubling. Teachers who have taken the important step of inviting students to help make up the rules would do well to question the value of generating a list of behavioral particulars—for at least three reasons. First of all, rules turn children into lawyers, scanning for loopholes and caveats, narrowing the discussion to technicalities when a problem occurs. The long-term implications of creating such a mind-set are quite disturbing, as Marilyn Watson explains:

> Students are encouraged to perform a kind of calculation: Is the fun or personal gain of this violation worth the pain or personal loss I'll suffer if I get caught? The school is seen as a legal system in which one operates out of self-interest, making personal choices

about one's behavior and experiencing the positive and negative consequences of such choices. In this case, the school is not a moral agent, not a socializing agent; it does not define the kind of community which the child is joining, but acts merely as an enforcer of an externally determined code of conduct, a code that is imposed on only some members: the students.[6]

Second, rules turn teachers into police officers, a role utterly at odds with being facilitators of learning. Watson again puts it very well:

> If adults are the upholders of order, then whenever they are in the presence of children, they must be vigilant. They must be watching for violations. . . . And most children will avoid the presence of adults for fear that they will be controlled or chastised. Such an approach to discipline creates the very opposite of a caring community—in fact, it mitigates against the school's becoming a community at all.

Third, rules usually enfold within them a punitive consequence for breaking them. The result is that we are thrown back into doing things *to* students rather than working *with* them to solve problems. The more "behavioral" or "black-and-white" the rule, the more likely it is that all these things will happen.

The alternative to concrete rules is not to say, "Do whatever you personally feel like." (That's another false dichotomy.) It is to engage the class in discussion about the "ways we want our class to be" (Child Development Project 1996a) and how that can be made to happen. There are few educational contrasts so sharp and meaningful as that between students being told what the teacher expects of them, what they are and are not permitted to do, and students coming together to reflect on how they can live and learn together. It is the difference between being prepared to spend a lifetime doing what one is told and being prepared to take an active role in a democratic society (or to transform a society *into* one that is democratic, as the case may be).

Do children differ in terms of their ability to think abstractly? Sure. Those who are inclined to think in concrete terms, if only because they are younger, can begin with specific ideas for how we should treat one another. But the process shouldn't end there. Working together to abstract a few common principles from a brain-stormed list of specific suggestions can be, among other things, a terrific way of honing thinking skills. It can help even six-year-olds to transcend a preoccupation with black-and-white rules. But first we educators have to do so.

## THE VALUE OF CONFLICT

The constructivist classroom, I have been arguing, is one in which the process matters at least as much as the product. The wrestling with dilemmas, the clash of ideas, the need to take others' needs into account—these are ultimately more meaningful than any list of rules or guidelines that may ultimately result. The sound of children arguing (at least in many circumstances) is music to the teacher's ears. Conflict is so vital to development that some experienced teachers go out of their way to highlight, or even create, situations where kids must think or feel their way out (Katz 1984, DeVries and Zan 1994, Lewis 1995), such as by deliberately having fewer materials available than there are children.

Of course, there is little need to invent conflict in many classrooms; the natural supply is abundant. Moreover, conflict sometimes takes forms that are patently destructive and must be stopped, if only to ensure the safety of the participants and those around them. But disagreement, however challenging it may be to the teacher and his prepared lesson plan, can be seen as an opportunity for learning—a teachable moment—rather than as something to be efficiently ended. Even unconstructive forms of conflict need to be resolved rather than snuffed out. (Unhappily, some versions of "conflict resolution" fail to live up to their name: they reflect little understanding of the need to examine the deeper issues involved, including people's motives—or the fact that something of value may have been gained because of the incident.)

Indeed, from this perspective there is something a little suspicious about classrooms that operate too smoothly, too cleanly. Here the conflict may have been pushed underground, or promptly dispatched by the teacher's intervention. Eric Schaps (1990, p. 8) expressed concern about classrooms he had observed where cooperative learn-

74

ing was going exactly according to plan, with students saying all the right things. "Deeper learning would look somewhat 'messier' than what I am seeing," he remarked, adding that many teachers "seem satisfied with easy or predictable answers. Their questions do not often probe or challenge; their comments are often routine and formulaic." If teachers and students were really exploring ideas wholeheartedly, there would be "more conflict, more frustration."

If two children are fussing with each other, the constructivist tries to resist the temptation to silence them or separate them in order to get on with the lesson. In an important sense, the conflict *is* the lesson—or at least it can become one if the teacher doesn't take over and solve (or end) the problem. But don't expect to find this point of view in discipline programs. Here, conflict is regarded as comparable to dandruff: something unsightly to be eliminated as rapidly as possible by using whatever seems to work.

To someone who thinks in terms of managing students, the only thing worse than the sort of conflict in which students are arguing with each other is the kind where they have the temerity to challenge the teacher. Thus, Cooperative Discipline tells us, a child's objections to something the teacher demands can be brushed off as "pseudologic" or "linguistic acrobatics" and need not be taken seriously (Albert 1989, p. 45). "Refuse to accept excuses," instructs Discipline with Dignity (Curwin and Mendler 1988, p. 15)—once again echoing the advice of Assertive Discipline (Canter and Canter 1992, p. 177). And from yet another source: a teacher who reprimands students for doing something must not listen if they attempt to explain what they were doing. The teacher must

> guard against . . . getting verbally engaged with the child about the particulars of the alibi. Such wheedling or diversionary tactics have as their sole purpose derailing your efforts to set a limit. If you do not bite the bait, you will succeed. Shut up, get close, and wait. When the child runs out of hot air, say firmly, "Sit up," "Turn around," or "Get to work." As soon as the child caves in and complies, become warm and nurturant and say, "Thank you" (Jones 1979, p. 29; also see Charney 1991, p. 102).

This advice appears in an article entititled "The Gentle Art of Class-room Discipline."

Such contempt for rational discourse with children—and indeed for children themselves, whose points of view are just so much "hot air"—follows naturally from the fact that a respectful dialogue may interfere with one's attempt to control them. It shows up again in the work of Dreikurs, notwithstanding his humanistic reputation. Over and over, he criticizes teachers for discussing problems rather than simply taking action. To discuss is to fall into the clever student's trap: "One cannot be firm if one talks. In the moment of conflict, talking is increased warfare and can have no beneficial effect" (Dreikurs and Grey 1968, p. 47). In place of discussion, the teacher who gets an argument from "the tyrant"—and this way of charac-terizing a student may tell us all we need to know about Dreikurs's point of view—should do the following: "first, you simply reply 'You may have a point.' Second, you do whatever *you* think is right" (Dreikurs and Cassel 1972, p. 69).

Unquestionably, there are some situations in the classroom that don't allow for an extended discussion at the time they occur. (A commitment to pick up the conversation later would seem to be called for here.) It's also true that some kinds of discussion are, shall we say, less useful than others. But the bottom line is that "teachers should expect and welcome children's excuses and arguments about rules" (Edwards 1986, p. 169) because that is how children become thinkers—by making up their own minds about whether something makes sense and figuring out how to convince others.

To discourage (let alone punish) objections is to sacrifice the development of judgment to the imperative of conformity. Denying students a voice, however, does not make their objections disappear; it just sweeps them under the carpet where people will trip over them—that is, where they will make their presence felt in ways that are less productive than rational argument.

Of course, it takes a special teacher to be open to this kind of conflict, someone who is not only patient but secure enough in her-self not to need to have the last word. Most of us will often find it difficult to welcome conflict, but this is surely something to which we can aspire. To create a classroom where students feel safe enough to challenge each other—and us—is to give them an enormous gift.

One more objection needs to be answered: Aren't there times when a student really is just trying to bait us or waste time? Yes, and it's certainly acceptable to suggest—gently and perhaps with a sense of humor—that this is what seems to be going on. But I trust teachers to be able to tell the difference if, as a rule, they welcome discussion and see conflict as desirable. I'm less sure about disciplinarians, with their deep suspicion of children's motives and their intolerance for dissent. Every challenge to them is likely to be seen as unacceptable; every question is impertinent.

Discipline writers may solemnly inform us that it is not enough to stop misbehavior in the classroom; rather, we must take action beforehand to limit its occurrence. But the real quantum leap in thinking is not from after-the-fact to prevention, where problems are concerned. It involves getting to the point that we ask, "What exactly is construed as a problem here—and why?" It means shifting from eliciting conformity and ending conflict to helping students become active participants in their own social and ethical development.

∞

# A CLASSROOM OF
# THEIR CHOOSING

The choice may have been mistaken,
The choosing was not.

—STEPHEN SONDHEIM, *SUNDAY IN THE PARK WITH GEORGE*

∞

## A TALE OF TWO TEACHERS

The construction of meaning is an active process. It can't be done unless the learner has substantial power to make decisions. If we are talking about learning to use the language, then those decisions include such issues as what to read and write about. If we are talking about learning to be a responsible, caring person, then the decisions include how to solve problems and get along with others.

Axiom: Students learn how to make good choices by making choices, not by following directions.

Corollary: Students will have little opportunity to do that kind of learning if teachers and administrators try to control or manage their behavior.

Let's meet two real teachers. The first is a 6th and 7th grade reading teacher in Oklahoma who makes up all the rules and insists that students obey them without question. These rules include:

- If Mrs. D_____ is talking, DON'T!
- If assigned, do it (on time, with a smile)!
- If you don't want to do it over, do it right the first time!

- If it's a school rule, follow it!
- If you gripe about the assignment, be prepared to do extra!

She elaborates on the last item:

> I don't want to hear, "Golly, two pages. Do we *have* to write two pages? What if we . . . ?" It's not "Let's Make a Deal" here. I'll just say, "Gee, I think you can write three or four pages on yours" (Dabney et al. 1994, pp. 63–64).

It isn't particularly remarkable for a teacher to shut students out of decision making—or even to threaten a punishment for asking, "What if we . . . ?"* What *is* remarkable here is that this teacher actually takes pride in stamping out dissent. She enthusiastically commends her approach to readers in a section of a book called *Innovative Discipline.*

The second teacher works at an elementary school in southern California and has come to a very different sort of relationship with students:

> I used to try to control students by asking my class leading questions in such a way that the children were forced into ritual answers that the teacher wanted. For example . . . I'd been lecturing the class about . . . getting in on time after recess. In the past I handled it in my usual way. They were always late lining up and I'd have to go out and yell at them to line up. By the time they all got there and lined up and walked to the room, we'd wasted at least ten minutes. When we got in the room, I'd say, "When the bell rings do we continue to play, class?" And they'd say, "No." . . . And the next day there I'd be, yelling at them to line up. . . .
>
> Well, this week . . . I told them how tired I was of yelling at them to line up and how afraid I was that the principal was going to give me a poor rating because of all the time we wasted. Then I listened to them. I couldn't believe my ears. They said they were sick of standing out there in the hot sun waiting for me and asked why they had to line up anyway. They couldn't

---

*Specifying that the punishment will be a longer assignment reveals quite a bit about the attitude toward learning in this classroom.

understand why they couldn't come to the room when the bell rang. I said that we'd always lined up, and they asked, "Why?" I thought about it for a while and then I said I couldn't think of any reason *why* students had to line up except that it was just the way things were done.

Well, they didn't buy that. We then decided to define our needs. Mine was to have them get from the playground to the classroom in an orderly, disciplined manner in as short a time as possible. Theirs was to avoid standing in a line for five or more minutes in the hot sun waiting for me to arrive to escort them to the classroom, and then having to march like soldiers. We decided on a solution suggested by one of the kids—namely, when the bell rang, they were to walk to the room from the playground. I was to walk from the teacher's lounge, and we'd go in. We've been trying it for three days now, and it's working beautifully (quoted in Gordon 1974, pp. 243–244).

This passage describes a breathtaking transformation, and I am not referring to the new plan for returning from recess. Everything in this classroom changed when the teacher stopped commanding and started listening, even if that happened only out of desperation. But this was just the beginning. No less important than letting students challenge the status quo was the teacher's willingness to admit that there may be no good reason for what had always been done, and (as a result) to reconsider the original request.

Finally, and perhaps most impressively, the students were not merely heard; they were invited to participate in formulating a solution. The result, we can assume, was not just that this classroom—in sharp contrast to the other teacher's—became a more pleasant place to spend the day; it also became a place where students could actively learn to be responsible people.

## WHY STUDENTS SHOULD HAVE A SAY

As Chapter 4 described, many classroom management programs use the language of choice against students as a kind of weapon: "You chose to misbehave" or even "You chose to be punished." What such programs conspicuously fail to provide is what students truly need: the chance to make real decisions about what happens in the classroom. Some of these decisions concern the academic part of their education—what to learn, and how, and why.[1] Here I focus instead on the role students can play in defining the broader contours of their life at school.

Why should we give them a chance to do so? There is no shortage of instrumental reasons—that is, ways in which choosing provides future benefits. But let's not forget that there is also an irreducible moral justification. Children are not just adults-in-the-making. They are people whose current needs and rights and experiences must be taken seriously. They ought to be able to make choices because people of any age ought to have some say about what happens to them (Chanoff 1981). How *much* say, and under what conditions, are open questions, of course. But the burden of proof rests with someone who wants to claim that a given individual in a given situation should be denied the chance to choose.

Having said that, we can move on to consider the practical advantages of letting students make decisions. The first benefit is that giving them some say will make it more likely that they will do essentially what we want. Choice promotes compliance and minimizes misbehavior. This is an important point for readers who, notwithstanding the previous chapter, are not quite ready to abandon the central goal of traditional discipline, even if they would just as soon avoid its methods (rewards and punishments).

Consider a rough syllogism. Major premise: children misbehave when their basic needs have not been met. Minor premise: children (like adults) have a basic need to experience themselves as "origins" of their own behavior as opposed to "pawns" (de Charms 1968, 1977). Conclusion: misbehavior will diminish when children feel less controlled. Kids tend to be more respectful when their need to make decisions is respected; they are likely to be better behaved when there is no need for them to struggle to assert their autonomy. Specifically, students are more likely to go along with a request, all things being equal, when they have some choice about how to carry it out.

The California elementary school teacher quoted above faced the problem of getting students back from recess without wasting too much time and decided to let the students themselves decide how to do that. But what will happen after the students return? What if they take five or ten minutes or more to get settled? The temptation, of course, is to try to manipulate their behavior with the usual methods:

• threatening punitive consequences ("Folks, if it takes as long to get seated after recess today as it did yesterday, you can forget about seeing that movie later"),

• threatening punitive consequences but pretending they're logical (". . . there won't be *time* for us to see that movie"),

• dangling collective rewards ("If everyone gets settled quickly after recess every day this week, we'll get to have a popcorn party on Friday!"), or

• holding up individual students as examples in order to control the behavior of everyone else ("I see that Marjorie is already in her seat! Who else is ready?").

Even if our goal is just to get students in their chairs quickly, giving them some choice in the matter is likely once again to be more effective than using bribes or threats. The teacher might invite some student(s) to monitor how long it's taking the class to get settled after recess, then ask everyone to reflect together on whether they need that much time, and finally solicit suggestions on how the process might be made more efficient. Later, she could check back with students to see whether the suggestions they agreed to try are working or could be improved.

The decision-making process here is driven solely by the teacher's short-term goal, which is to get the students to sit down. Moreover, the process only allows them to decide *how* to make that happen, not whether to do so. We would hope that not all choices for children would be so sharply circumscribed, but to present some that way, to offer a broad framework inside which students can make decisions, does make sense some of the time. The key is to

82

make sure that we are always offering a real choice ("How do you think we can get settled more quickly?") and not a pseudochoice of the kind so commonly prescribed in discipline plans ("Do you want to get settled right away or do you want to do without the movie?"). (See Chapter 4.)

Also, by virtue of being a "working with" solution, bringing students in on the process is likely to work a lot better than the "doing to" techniques that come to mind so readily. In this sense, giving students more control over their lives, more choices about how things are done in the classroom, can indeed be filed under "Discipline, Practical Alternatives to."

Another reason to let students choose is to help each of them become *self*-disciplined. But that term can be used in different ways, and we need to look carefully at the context to figure out what it really means. It can signify a much more ambitious goal than compliance—or it can be just a different way of talking about compliance. When some people describe a student as self-disciplined, they mean only that she does what is expected even when no adult is watching (or giving out rewards or punishments). The goal here is just to get the student to keep acting in ways that are acceptable to us, which amounts to trying to direct her behavior by remote control.

To be sure, giving students some say about how they act can help make that happen. But there is a big difference between "internal" and "intrinsic" (Ryan, Koestner, and Deci 1991), between internalizing values and constructing them (Piaget 1965, Kamii et al. 1994)—in short, between being self-disciplined (in this limited sense of the term) and truly autonomous. Accepting someone else's expectations is a far cry from developing one's own. Doing something out of a sense of compulsion isn't at all the same thing as doing it because one knows and feels that it is the right thing to do. The ultimate reason to give children a say is that it can help them to make their own good decisions, to grow into ethical and compassionate people—not because it will make them internalize what we want them to do. Our decisions about *how* we involve them in making decisions should be guided by what helps that to happen.

# BEYOND SELF-DISCIPLINE

Here is another story about coming back from recess: a 2nd grade teacher, returning to her classroom after a break, discovered many of her students already back in the room, animatedly discussing something among themselves. When she asked them what was going on, they informed her that a problem had come up during recess and they were holding a class meeting to solve it—which they proceeded to do while she finished her coffee across the room.[2]

"Self-disciplined" children might come back from recess promptly without having to be goaded or reminded. *These* children, by contrast, were self-directed, possessed of both the skills and the inclination to solve their problem autonomously. Carefully measured dollops of choice are useful for achieving the former. A truly autonomy-supporting classroom is necessary for achieving the latter.

The creation of such classrooms, however, depends on teachers who pointedly decline to lay down the law and take control. By "refus[ing] to be all knowing or all powerful, they open the way for children to struggle with issues and not rely on adults for truths and values" (DeVries and Zan 1994, p. 193). The difficulty of relinquishing power, or of realizing the importance of doing so, is evident from the number of adults who spend their days ordering children around, complaining all the while that "kids just don't take responsibility for their own behavior." The truth is that if we want children to *take* responsibility, we must first *give* them responsibility, and plenty of it. As Constance Kamii (1991, p. 398) has written,

> We cannot expect children to accept ready-made values and truths all the way through school, and then suddenly make choices in adulthood. Likewise, we cannot expect them to be manipulated with reward and punishment in school, and to have the courage of a Martin Luther King in adulthood.

In fact, an emphasis on following instructions, respecting authority (regardless of whether that respect has been earned), and obeying the rules (regardless of whether they are reasonable) teaches a disturbing lesson. Stanley Milgram's famous experiment, in which ordinary people gave what they thought were terribly painful shocks to hapless strangers merely because they were told to do so by someone in charge, is not just a comment about "society" or "human nature." It is a cautionary tale about certain ways of teaching children.

To talk about the importance of choice is also to talk about democracy. At present, as Shelley Berman (1990, p. 2) of Educators for Social Responsibility has drily noted, "We teach reading, writing, and math by [having students do] them, but we teach democracy by lecture." Anyone who truly values democratic ideals would presumably want to maximize children's experiences with choice and negotiation.

Studies support this view. Students who are able to participate in making decisions at school are more committed to decision making and democracy in other contexts (D'Amico 1980, Battistoni 1985, Angell 1991). Another line of research, meanwhile, suggests that when we look inside the classrooms of teachers who are less controlling and more inclined to support children's autonomy, we find students who are more self-confident and more interested in learning for its own sake (Deci, Nezlek, and Sheinman 1981). Clearly, the case for student participation is compelling.

# STRUCTURE VS. CONTROL

A teacher once told me how much her students' morale had improved when she started letting them read or write in any position they chose—sitting, standing, or lying down anywhere in the room. That struck me as a little bit depressing because it pointed up how the norm is to deny students even the most basic control over their own bodies. A choice that children should be able to make as a matter of course is the exception rather than the rule.

Each aspect of life in a classroom offers an invitation to think about what decisions might be turned over to students—or negotiated with students—individually and collectively. The fact that some child might take advantage of the chance to decide when to go to the bathroom is no justification for requiring everyone to ask permission. If it's useful to keep track of who's out of the room, or to limit the number who are gone at any given time, children can take a pass

85

or sign out when they feel the need. Better yet, they can be asked as a class to invent a system that addresses everyone's concerns—theirs for autonomy, the teacher's for structure or limits.

Notice that these are not mutually exclusive goals, provided that the structures or limits are reasonable. The less reasonable they are, the more they come to resemble old-fashioned control. This important distinction (e.g., Deci and Ryan 1985, 1990) seems to elude a number of people in the fields of classroom management and special education: the talk is all about the need for structures or limits, but the prescribed interventions are designed for control. Here are half a dozen criteria for determining how defensible a given structure or limit is—or, conversely, how much it has begun to resemble control.

• **Purpose.** A restriction would be more legitimate if, for example, its objective were to protect children from hurting themselves as opposed to imposing order for its own sake.

• **Restrictiveness.** The less restrictive, the better. It's harder to justify a demand for silence than for quiet voices, or for banning certain items that might become messy as opposed to asking that the room be kept clean.

• **Flexibility.** It makes sense to give the day some structure— the morning in an elementary classroom might start with an hour for work on science projects before beginning partner reading—but it's also important to be able to modify that schedule depending on what happens during the science period.

• **Developmental appropriateness.** It's one thing to make sure that a four-year-old has dressed for winter weather, and something quite different to monitor the clothing of a ten-year-old.

• **Presentation style.** Although it is far from the only criterion, the way a given restriction or requirement is introduced to students can make a difference. An interesting study found that there were no negative effects when guidelines for using art supplies were presented respectfully, with the adult acknowledging children's feelings (that cleaning up after oneself can be a nuisance) and offering a rationale for the guidelines. But when the identical rules were presented to another group of children in a controlling tone—essentially

86

ordering them to comply—these children showed less interest in painting and actually did less creative work (Koestner, Ryan, Bernieri, and Holt 1984).

- **Student Involvement.** Finally, and most importantly, what distinguishes an acceptable classroom structure from a mechanism of control is the input that students have. The relevant question, as Thomas Gordon (1989, p. 9) emphasizes, is not whether limits or rules are necessary, but "Who sets them: the adults alone or the adults and kids—together?"

This last point brings us back to students' need for autonomy. Even though the teacher can print more neatly, children should have the chance to write their own names on cards that identify their lockers or coat hooks or desks, or to sign in each morning rather than having the teacher take attendance. (Besides, it doesn't hurt to give young children practice at writing.) Even though it's easier to maintain order by marking out the area of the floor to be used for circle time—or assigning children specific places to sit—even preschoolers should be able to find their own spots. (Besides, it doesn't hurt to give them practice at solving conflicts, should any develop.)

If we're not ready to give students a completely open-ended free period, we can at least offer them several options for how to spend a certain chunk of time each day. If we're not ready to leave it up to two warring students to take the initiative to make peace, we can at least bring them together and pointedly ask them, "What do you think you can do to solve this problem?" If they have no ideas, we can propose some possibilities from which they can choose. If they need the teacher's help, the question might become, "What do you think *we* can do to solve this problem?"

And so on.

# TO MEET NEEDS, WE NEED TO MEET

For the questions that affect most, if not all, of the class, the best forum is the class meeting (Glasser 1969, chaps. 10–12; Gordon 1974, chaps. 8–9; Nelsen et al. 1993; Child Development Project 1996a):

- This is the place for *sharing*—for example, talking about interesting things that happened over the weekend. (Don't confuse sharing with the conventional and often competitive ritual known as Show and Tell, which Lilian Katz has dubbed "Bring and Brag." Students should decide when they want to participate rather than feeling compelled to produce something; moreover, the idea is to take pleasure in others' contributions rather than trying to outdo them.)

- This is the place for *deciding*—for example, how best to help people in need, rather than just taking part in established holiday charity rituals. Class meetings are also ideal for making decisions about more basic matters, such as how to decorate the walls. Of course, if students are to make this particular decision, the walls should be bare on the first day of school. One 3rd grade teacher told me that it took several summers before she finally summoned the nerve to not decorate her classroom. The feel of her class was much more positive that year, she reported, possibly because the children experienced the classroom, in the most literal sense, as their own.[3] In a 6th grade classroom in Arizona, the students were asked in a class meeting to figure out how they wanted the furniture arranged, and they opted to cluster the desks in groups. At a later meeting, they concluded that the arrangement wasn't working very well and decided to move the desks up against the walls; they wanted to have somewhere to do their individual work while leaving the bulk of the room open for teamwork, meetings, and various projects.

- This is the place for *planning*—for example, figuring out how to make a field trip happen: getting permission, raising money, arranging for food, inviting chaperons, and so forth. In my experience, even seasoned and democratically oriented teachers never stop discovering such opportunities: "Wait a minute! I could be bringing the students in on making this decision—or following through on this task—even though I've always just taken care of it myself."

- This is the place for *reflecting*—for example, about what kind of place the classroom should be. At the beginning of the year—and then from time to time as necessary—students might talk about the values they believe should inform their life together and the rationale for doing things a certain way. How should we treat each other? What can we do when we don't agree, or when somebody says or does something unpleasant? What happens when the obligation of the community to set norms of kindness clashes with the right of individuals to choose their friends (Paley 1992)? How come the teacher doesn't give us stickers when we're "good"—the way last year's teacher did? Why exactly do we spend time learning in groups instead of just alone, or reading aloud, or doing math? ("Whether or not we acknowledge it, students are curriculum theorists and critics of schooling. If they are drawn into the conversation about the purposes and practices of schooling, we may all learn useful lessons" [Nicholls and Hazzard 1993, p. 8].)

Consider a concrete example in which many of these strands come together. The teacher knows he is going to be absent for the next few days. Assume he wants to transcend the usual "doing to" tactics: "If I get a bad report from the substitute, here's what will happen to you" or "If I get a good report, here's what I'll give you." How might he work *with* the students to head off potential problems? (I've found that this question often leads to a spirited discussion at a faculty meeting or staff development session—not only generating specific ideas but also helping participants think through the difference between "doing to" and "working with.")

The teacher, of course, could call a class meeting to announce that a sub will be coming and to make sure that everyone can recite what he expects of them. But this is just an exercise in control dressed up as a class meeting. Far better would be to ask the students what *they* think might be useful for making sure that the days he is away will be spent productively. Maybe they could work together to plan the curriculum for when he is gone. Or maybe he could present the discussion as a brainstorming session on how we can make this stranger feel welcome in our room. (This way, the challenge is framed as helping a guest rather than obeying a surrogate authority figure.) Inviting students to reflect on how things might look from the sub's point of view can facilitate that kind of discussion: Will she know anyone here? How does it feel when you don't know anyone, but everyone else knows each other?

The students may suggest, and rightly so, that the teacher should try to speak to the sub beforehand, not just to pass on a lesson plan but to discuss how things work in this classroom: how community is valued over compliance, what decisions are usually made by the students, why rewards and punishments aren't used, and so forth. Finally, another class meeting might be scheduled for when the teacher returns—not for pointing fingers or imposing consequences, but for a thoughtful discussion about how things went and how they might be improved the next time the teacher is absent (Child Development Project 1996a, pp. 72–75, 94–96).

It sounds easier than it is, this business of holding class meetings. Sometimes participants can't agree on a solution. Does that mean we carry the item over to the next meeting—or have we done something sufficiently constructive just by raising the issue and airing our ideas and feelings? Sometimes students don't participate. Shall we break into pairs to talk, or write down our individual responses, and then come back together to share our new proposals? Or might people be getting something of value from the discussion even when they don't contribute? Sometimes students snicker unkindly at someone's idea, or don't pay attention, or let a couple of their peers effectively take over the meeting. These are not problems for the teacher to solve alone; they are issues to be folded back into the meeting and dealt with by its members.

How do you find the time for these meetings when they cut into the already scarce hours allotted to academics? You make the time. Apart from the invaluable social and ethical benefits of class meetings, they foster intellectual development as well, as students learn to reason their way through problems, analyzing possibilities and negotiating solutions. Besides, students who participate in shaping their own schooling are likely to be less alienated and more effective learners the rest of the day. And less time will be wasted on discipline in such a classroom.

That's why one secondary math teacher in Massachusetts[4] regularly devotes time to class meetings even though he, like his students, is a prisoner of the absurd traditional high school schedule that divides the day into 45-minute periods of unrelated subjects. During these meetings, students can reflect on how the class is going, exchange ideas on their independent projects, decide collectively when the next test should be scheduled, discuss whether it makes more sense to go over last night's homework as a class or in small groups (where, as one boy observes, you "can't not do anything"), or argue about whether it's fair for someone to get a low grade for the course despite scoring high on the tests.

It is immediately clear to someone who visits this class that students learn math more enthusiastically in the time that remains than they would if the race to cover the curriculum superseded the chance to talk about how things are going. Asked to reflect on this course, one student remarks that "it's more oriented to *us*" than other classes are. Someone else adds that the student-directed model leads to "learning" rather than just "remembering." And a third student describes how difficult this approach was for her initially, since she was someone who preferred to be told what to do. At first, she says, "I couldn't really deal with sitting in a circle and talking stuff to death," but by the spring, "I was, like, starting to take responsibility."

## MEETINGS FOR BETTER OR WORSE

Perhaps the most common, and persistent, question faced by teachers who facilitate class meetings is when to speak up and when to shut up, when to pose a question or offer an observation and when to let the students do it themselves. The answer is that there is no answer—at least, no formula that can be applied across the board. It is much easier to specify what *not* to do: don't run the whole show.

There are well-meaning manuals on how to create a responsive classroom community in which the suggested activities—including class meetings—leave very little for the students to do, apart from waiting for the teacher to call on them so they can answer questions that she has posed. Indeed, there are teachers who pride themselves on holding class meetings even though what they are doing scarcely deserves that name.

In a 3rd grade classroom in New Jersey, I once watched a teacher whose approach to academic instruction could be described as a model of student-centered discovery and constructivist learning. I was genuinely impressed. Then the class meeting began. "Where do you sit?" she asked one boy—and then cut him off as he started to answer, chasing him back to his assigned seat. The meeting's purpose was to discuss a scheduled field trip, but it consisted mostly of her telling students what she thought they needed to know. "What do we have to do before the trip?" she asked. Students offered several suggestions, which were brushed aside until she got the answer she wanted ("plan the route") and wrote that one on a flip chart.

The point throughout the meeting was to be the first to guess what was on the teacher's mind, with the predictable result that students periodically accused one another of stealing their answers. She reprimanded them when they shouted out responses, and at one point announced, "I am very unhappy with some people's behavior. This is such a smart group, I don't think I need to explain. Well, maybe I do for Bryan and Danny." Later, without warning, she expelled someone from the circle for talking.

I have seen "class meetings" even more tightly controlled—indeed, more punitive—than this one, but here the lesson in contrasts was memorable. Deep thinking did, in fact, take place in this classroom whenever it was time for math or reading. But outside of academics, the teacher might as well have been using Assertive Discipline. At no point during the meeting had students been asked to make a decision or think through an issue or even address each other.

It seems quite paradoxical: "a curriculum that urges problem solving and critical thinking and a management system that requires compliance and narrow obedience." But it is more than a paradox: it is ultimately an "oxymoron," because classroom management of this type "dilutes, if not obstructs, the potential power of the curriculum for many of our students" (McCaslin and Good 1992, p. 12). As Connie Kamii and her colleagues (1994, p. 677) explain, "A classroom cannot foster the development of autonomy in the intellectual realm while suppressing it in the social and moral realms."

About a month after visiting that 3rd grade classroom, I found myself in a kindergarten in Missouri where the children's ideas and questions were taken seriously, even outside of formal lessons. This was a place where the teacher paused before erasing a childish scrawl on the blackboard to ask whether it was something important enough to be saved. It was a place where the teacher was not the only one authorized to flick the light switch when she had an important announcement to make; the students had that right, too.

The point of the meeting I happened to observe was to decide whether rules were needed for playing Legos. In anticipation of the meeting, a few budding architects had proposed guidelines, which a girl had written down in a language only she was able to decipher. A discussion ensued about each rule and its rationale. Particularly controversial was a suggested prohibition on copying someone else's idea about what to build. The teacher skillfully introduced the meta-question of whether everyone must submit to a single policy or whether it might be legitimate to ban "copycatting" the work of only those who objected to it. A discussion and vote followed.

Down the hall from this kindergarten was a 2nd grade classroom[5] where it took me a few seconds to find the teacher. (Experience suggests this is usually a very good sign.) These seven-year-olds were running their own class meeting to solve a series of problems. Today's facilitator—a role that all students fill on a rotating basis, I later learned—kept watch over the agenda. When a topic was finished, she consulted the list and invited the person who had suggested the next item to come up and sit in a big rocking chair at the front of the room. He or she explained the issue, at which point the facilitator invited questions or proposals, while another student, standing in front of a whiteboard, laboriously recorded what was said.

The children sat on the floor, on chairs, on tables, or wherever they were comfortable. The teacher sat with them and sometimes raised her hand to be recognized, just as they did. At this particular meeting, she spoke only once or twice during a meeting that lasted fully two hours. When someone started to ramble, the facilitator gently guided him or her back to the topic by asking, "Is that our problem?"

One girl, when called to the rocking chair, announced that other kids were picking on her during Four Square, a playground game.

Various suggestions were offered in response, ranging from trying to ignore those kids to telling a grown-up. During the discussion, children periodically reminded each other to raise their hands and also to avoid mentioning names when complaining about someone else's behavior. As in the kindergarten class, an interesting meta-issue emerged, this time without the teacher's help: Must all participants (or a majority) agree on which solution is best, or was the group's responsibility limited to offering possibilities to the girl with the problem, who would be free to pick whichever one seemed to work for her? One got the impression throughout this complicated conversation that nothing about the proceedings, including the children's earnest attention to what was going on, would have changed if the teacher were suddenly to stand up and leave the room.

## REFLECTIONS ON DECISION MAKING

Classrooms like the latter two are not unusual in some parts of the world. For example, despite Japan's reputation for a system that overwhelms teenagers with academic pressure, early childhood education there is characterized by free play, an emphasis on caring, and the opportunity for children to make meaningful decisions. Teachers routinely try "to provoke children to come up with solutions to problems—even when this [takes] many minutes of class time." They not only avoid controlling students' behavior with rewards[6] or punishments, but even shy away from making "authoritative statements that might short-circuit children's own problem solving." Deeply reflective class meetings are the norm (Lewis 1995, pp. 28, 113).

I don't know how many such classrooms exist in the United States. Plainly they are in the minority, but whatever their number, each offers a ringing refutation of the charge that it is "unrealistic" to give children more autonomy or to move beyond a focus on compliance and traditional discipline. Making that journey is often difficult and even frightening, but it is as possible as it is desirable.

The responsible, caring children one meets in such classrooms did not drop down from some teacher heaven. What mostly distinguishes them is their teachers—and, by extension, the administrative support offered for such teaching. When young children take responsibility for solving their problems, or even spontaneously convene their own meetings during recess, you can bet that the teacher worked awfully hard over a period of months to help them get to that point. He or she did not just *let* them make decisions, but actively supported their autonomy, inviting participation and teaching them the necessary skills.

There are good ways of doing this, and there are even better ways. For example, it is good to give students the chance to pick their favorite option from a list of possibilities. It is better when they can sometimes *generate* the possibilities.

It is good when students get to vote rather than being told what to do. It is better when they are encouraged to hash out a consensus together or reach a compromise. Voting is just "adversarial majoritarianism"—a contest that produces losers who often have no commitment to what the larger number of participants want. More important, the hard work of listening, considering others' points of view, and fashioning new solutions—in short, the guts of democracy—is all but absent when matters are just put to a vote.[7] (For a practical guide on how to help students reach consensus, see Child Development Project 1996a, pp. 36–41.)

It is good when class meetings provide a chance for students to come together and make decisions. It is better when the approach that defines class meetings is reflected throughout the rest of the day as well. We don't want to ritualize meetings and set them apart: we want much of the interaction and learning that takes place in a classroom to resemble the democratic activity that goes on in meetings.

It is good when students can meet as a class to make decisions. It is better when they can also meet on a schoolwide basis. (Here I do not include traditional student councils, which suffer from at least three weaknesses: only a few get to participate, students are set against each other in a competition to decide who those few will be, and decisions of real significance are rarely part of their purview. Even in high school, the agenda is more likely to include social events than school governance.)

It is good when older students have the chance to make decisions. It is better when younger ones, too, get that opportunity. Of course, children can handle more freedom and make better choices as they get older. Who could deny that a 16-year-old can approach a decision in a more sophisticated way than a 6-year-old, and therefore can usually be entrusted with more responsibility? But this fact is sometimes used to justify preventing younger children from making choices that are well within their capabilities. (That's why I have deliberately mentioned classrooms where the children are no older than seven.) Moreover, the idea that we have to wait until children are mature enough to handle responsibilities may set up a vicious circle: it is experience with decisions that helps children *become* capable of handling them.

On the other hand, if students have been abruptly freed from control—if they are being asked to make decisions after years of being required (by parents or other teachers) to do what they are told—they may need some time to get used to this. Just as it takes the eyes a moment to adjust to the sunny outdoors after emerging from a dark room, so it takes the mind and heart a while to cope with freedom after having been expected to do what one is told.

In fact, students may respond to such a shift in any of several ways that can be discouraging for educators who aren't prepared for these reactions:

• **Acting out.** During a transitional period, you may see a lot more behavior of every kind, including negative behavior, that had hitherto been squelched. This is not especially pleasant, but the slogan to keep in mind is "Bring the kids in on it." As with other problems, it is something that the whole class should address. Ask students if they can figure out what's going on—and what to do about it. It may be that you are overwhelming them with choices and need to go slower in the transition away from control.

• **Testing.** Like misbehavior, outrageous suggestions in a class meeting can sometimes be a way of testing you. The usual interpretation of this behavior, which is suspiciously convenient for those who prefer conventional practices, is that children are really asking for limits and discipline. But consider the possibility that they are testing you to see whether you mean what you say when you tell them their needs and preferences matter. They may be asking you to prove that you are not just a teacher who reassuringly declares, "This is *our* classroom!". . . and then proceeds to keep all the important decisions for herself.

• **Outright resistance.** You ask students what to do about a particular problem and someone replies sullenly, "That's your job. You're the teacher." Do you feel resentful, as though these kids don't even appreciate the marvelous gift of freedom you've given them? Better, if you can manage it, is a reaction of excitement: What an invitation to reflect together about these issues! You might ask them, "What *is* the teacher's job? And what about yours? Are you old enough to participate in such decisions? Do you learn better in a classroom where someone is always telling you what to do?"

• **Silence.** Sometimes students do not take part in a class meeting, or they offer nothing more responsive than "I dunno" or "Whatever" when asked individually for their opinion. As usual, the behavior is much less important than the reason for it. The teacher's first job is to figure out why this is happening. Nothing to say for the moment? Doesn't feel safe with you (or other classmates)? Chronic shyness? Trouble handling the new responsibility? Naturally, each of these calls for a different course of action (or inaction).

• **Parroting.** Students unaccustomed to making decisions, more concerned about pleasing the teacher than thinking, may go through the motions while offering the sort of responses calculated to make you happy. The trick is to not be happy. One is tempted to react with pleasure when the very rule or idea or answer you had in mind comes out of a student's mouth. But this is not successful participation; it is ventriloquism.

If you ask the class how they might help others to learn, and someone instantly replies, "Respect other people's needs," you might want to invite deeper reflection rather than taking that response at face value—taking care, of course, not to criticize the student who dutifully recited what he had heard. "What exactly does it mean to be respectful?" you might ask. "Why is it important?" "Does everyone agree?" More generally, you could ask students about their experiences with saying what they knew would please an adult and how different that feels from taking the risk of making a suggestion that someone might not like. Then emphasize that the latter is what you are looking for here.

Of course, this approach assumes that the latter *is* what you are looking for here. Often children have a tough time thinking for themselves because the adult has mixed feelings about their doing so.

## BAD DECISIONS

What if students welcome, rather than resist, the opportunity to make decisions—and then make one you think is terrible? It depends how strongly you feel and on what you base your disapproval. If there are some decisions you simply cannot live with—as there are for all of us—then make that clear from the beginning. Even worse than no choice at all is a situation where students are led to think they can decide, only to learn afterward that because they didn't make the "right" choice, their participation was, in effect, a charade.

Let's say that a student wants to know why everyone must raise his or her hand before speaking. The worst possible response would be, "Because that's the rule. Now get back to work." Somewhat better would be to throw the question back to that student ("Why do *you* think?"), or invite others to answer, in the hope that they will come up with the "correct" response ("So that everyone doesn't talk at once") and then be satisfied with the status quo.

Best of all would be to invite a real discussion whose conclusion cannot be predicted. Imagine that such a discussion is underway, and there is a clear consensus for getting rid of the hand-raising ritual. Someone (you, if necessary) will raise the possibility that discussions may become chaotic. So a student proposes the following alternative: "People who want to talk can just go, 'Beep beep!' before they say anything." You ask whether others regard this as a workable idea, hoping that they will see its flaws. But instead there is overwhelming enthusiasm. What do you do?

You say, "Well, let's give it a try—and then let's check back in a day or two to see how it's working." The benefits of letting students decide far outweigh the disadvantages of implementing a silly proposal.

Imagine that you ask your class for suggestions on where to take a field trip. Someone suggests France, and students cheer. What do you do? That depends on whether you think they are serious. If not, respond humorously ("But why? We can get french fries right here"). If students are serious, you have a wonderfully teachable moment, a chance to help them think about where France is, what it would take to get there, and so on.

Sometimes you will be genuinely torn between, on the one hand, honoring their choice even though you find it disturbing and, on the other hand, sacrificing their autonomy in the name of a value that is just too important. (Administrators committed to supporting the autonomy of teachers face the same dilemma when teachers choose to do hurtful things to children.) What if students decide, in effect, that they don't want to decide (Lickona and Paradise 1980)? Suppose you ask them how they want the class to be managed and they go with what they know: a carrot-and-stick system such as Assertive Discipline. One 5th grade teacher from Georgia found himself in that very situation and reluctantly decided to respect the students' wishes.

> The class used Assertive Discipline for a month before becoming dissatisfied with it. They felt that it did not help them accomplish their main goal of behaving responsibly. They did not like putting names on the board and noticed that the same names were always there. They voted to modify the system by placing color strips on the culprit's desk. Soon, however, they came to realize that they preferred a system not tied to external rewards [and punishments] (Bloom and Herzog 1994, p. 206).

It would be interesting to know how this teacher framed the initial question that led students to choose Assertive Discipline. Problematic decisions can often be attributed to problematic questions. If we ask students what should happen to people who break our rules, they will sometimes respond by proposing hair-raisingly harsh punishments. But notice that the question implicitly accepts a traditional discipline framework. Had the students been invited to think outside of that box, to reflect on alternatives to "doing to" tactics, then the dilemma of whether to implement their troubling suggestion might not have arisen.

Of course, it can be just as hard for adults to think in unfamiliar terms as it is for children. Educators who have spent years pursuing the goals and practices described earlier in this book ought not to expect a rapid conversion to democratic teaching. For teachers who are themselves controlled by administrators, the task may be even more difficult. On one level, it seems ironic that teachers who complain bitterly about having to turn in lesson plans, adopt a certain discipline program, or attend specified inservice events—in short, those who resent being deprived of autonomy—often turn around and treat their students exactly the same way, tightly regulating their behavior.

On another level, this behavior is not ironic at all; it is exactly what we would expect. "When teachers are treated as pawns, they don't teach, they become drill sergeants" (de Charms 1977, p. 444). Sure enough, researchers have discovered that when teachers are pressured to improve students' performance on tests, they tend to act in more controlling ways with students, giving them less choice than do teachers who are free to facilitate students' learning (Deci et al. 1982).

For administrators to share power with teachers, and teachers with students, is to undertake a monumental challenge. But we might well ask about the long-term implications of *denying* people a role in the decisions that affect them. Winston Churchill's remark during a speech to the House of Commons half a century ago should resonate with educators today: "It has been said that democracy is the worst form of government—except all those other forms that have been tried from time to time."

∞

# Chapter 7

# THE CLASSROOM
# AS COMMUNITY

The evident weakness in American schools has much to do
with the weakening of their community context. . . .
Education can never merely be for the sake of individual
self-enhancement. It pulls us into the common world or it
fails altogether.

—ROBERT BELLAH ET AL., *THE GOOD SOCIETY*

∽

## WHY COMMUNITY?

For all the talk one hears in certain educational circles about the
importance of creating "communities," few people indicate precisely
what that term means. Perhaps they find it difficult to nail down the
concept; like Justice Powell struggling to define *pornography,* they
may resort to saying that they know it when they see it.

But I think we can do better. Indeed, we have an obligation to
specify what this idea means if we are proposing that it should guide
our work. In saying that a classroom or school is a "community,"
then, I mean that it is a place in which students feel cared about and
are encouraged to care about each other. They experience a sense
of being valued and respected; the children matter to one another
and to the teacher. They have come to think in the plural: they
feel connected to each other; they are part of an "us." And, as a

result of all this, they feel safe in their classes, not only physically but emotionally.

To say that a classroom is a community, in other words, is to say that it is a place where

> care and trust are emphasized above restrictions and threats, where unity and pride (of accomplishment and in purpose) replace winning and losing, and where each person is asked, helped, and inspired to live up to such ideals and values as kindness, fairness, and responsibility. [Such] a classroom community seeks to meet each student's need to feel competent, connected to others, and autonomous. . . . Students are not only exposed to basic human values, they also have many opportunities to think about, discuss, and act on those values, while gaining experiences that promote empathy and understanding of others (Child Development Project 1991).

In recent years, more educators have begun to pay attention to these dimensions of schooling. Thomas J. Sergiovanni (1994, p. xi) has gone so far as to declare that "community building must become the heart of any school improvement effort." After all, how many children can grow—intellectually, emotionally, or any other way—without a supportive environment? Virtually any meaningful long-term goal we might have for students requires us to attend to the climate of the school and, specifically, the extent to which children feel related, as opposed to isolated.

Some of the most important work on formulating, researching, and implementing the idea of caring communities has been done in connection with an elementary school program called the Child Development Project (Battistich et al. 1989; Watson et al. 1989; Kohn 1990c; Solomon et al. 1992). The staff of the CDP, based in Oakland, California, has worked in eight school districts both within and beyond California to promote students' social, moral, and intellectual development.[1] The definition of community cited just above comes from the CDP, and in fact the whole of this book reflects the impact of this group's work: it has profoundly shaped my thinking about what ought to happen in schools, about how a caring community can be constructed as well as why it is so important to do so.

The rationale for promoting community is powerfully evident from a recent CDP study of two dozen elementary schools around the country. Students in the upper grades were asked about the extent to which they experienced their classroom and school as supportive communities. It turned out that the stronger that community feeling was, the more the students reported liking school and the more they saw learning as something valuable in its own right. These students also tended to be more concerned about others and more skilled at resolving conflict than those who didn't feel part of a community. What's more, these positive effects were particularly pronounced in schools that had more low-income students (Battistich et al. 1995).

The CDP study suggests that taking the time to help children care about each other might just affect their enthusiasm about academic learning. That is an insight with the potential to reshape the whole enterprise of school reform, but it really shouldn't be surprising. Students need to feel safe in order to take intellectual risks; they must be comfortable before they can venture into the realm of discomfort. Few things stifle creativity like the fear of being judged or humiliated. Thus, a supportive environment will allow people of any age to play with possibilities and challenge themselves to stretch their thinking. The moral is: if you want academic excellence, you have to attend to how children feel about school and about each other.

Note that the CDP study also supports the idea that students in communities are better at conflict resolution and more likely to care about others. This finding is consistent with the work of Piaget (1965) and other researchers who have argued that cooperative relationships among children are the key to moral development. Each member of a community has the opportunity to see things as they appear to others, and in so doing to think in a way that is deeper and less self-centered.

Another way of emphasizing the importance of community is to point out how difficult it is to do other things of value without it. Three examples should illustrate the point.

- "When a spirit of cooperative community is missing, 'democratic' [class] meetings can become merely a forum for pressing and

103

defending one's narrow self-interest" (Lickona and Paradise 1980, p. 334). Of course, these meetings can themselves help to build and support that cooperative spirit, but it is important that they are construed from the beginning as activities by and for *us*. A meeting should be experienced as one important way that our community shares and decides, plans and reflects. Otherwise, it may come to resemble something closer to a courtroom, where individuals press their case against one another: a meeting of the "mines."

• Multi-age classrooms and cross-age activities are enormously useful; they have the potential to promote generosity as well as better thinking skills for both the older and younger children involved (Foot et al. 1990; Pavan 1992; Child Development Project 1996b). How, then, do we explain the complaints that in some of these classrooms the younger children are teased or excluded? The likely culprit is a failure to create a community, to promote a sense of connection and caring. Unfortunately, some teachers or parents may be inclined to reject the whole idea of multi-age education rather than embracing the idea of community to make it work.

• I visited a well-known free school in Massachusetts not long ago, a place where students not only direct their own learning but decide when and whether to have a lesson. Yet discipline in this stunningly unconventional school is suspiciously familiar: it consists of an intricate welter of bylaws, along with a Justice Committee to enforce them by meting out punishments to those found guilty of wrongdoing. To be sure, the process here is distinctive by virtue of the fact that power rests in the hands of students. But one is led to wonder why the school is still stuck on the traditional arrangement of threats and punishments to deal with conflicts.

After some reflection, I concluded that a move from "doing to" to "working with" is impossible unless there has been an effort to create and sustain relationships among the people involved. The alternative to discipline is to treat an inappropriate act as a problem to be solved together—but that is predicated on the experience of *being* together. With nothing more than a loosely confederated bunch of free individuals, one is left with the same old rules-and-penalties model. The pursuit of laissez-faire liberty condemns us to a system of control, even though different people may be doing the controlling.

Autonomy is not enough; we need community, too.

# OBJECTIONS TO COMMUNITY

The idea of community at first seems so bland and unobjectionable that support for it might almost be dismissed as hollow rhetoric. On closer inspection, though, it represents a radical and disconcerting challenge to much of what we take for granted. This is true because it calls into question several overlapping aspects of the status quo.

When we talk about "discipline," for example, we are talking about how the adult intervenes with this student or that one. Moreover, the intervention—like the usual view of teaching itself—is often conceived as instilling something in, or transmitting something to, each student. Even people committed to cooperative learning often see their mission as changing each participant into someone who can listen, make eye contact, encourage others, and so forth.

The community approach goes beyond teacher-student interaction and asks us to consider the broader question of how everyone gets along together. It also suggests that the way students turn out is a function not only of what each has been taught, but of how their environment has been set up. If we want to help children grow into compassionate people, we have to help them change the way the classroom works and feels, not just the way each separate member of that class acts. We have to transform not just individuals but educational *structures*.

The structural approach has another interesting implication: caring is more than just a characteristic of teachers. Obviously it's very important that the adults in a school be generous, warm people. But it's just as vital to attend to how the classroom or school is arranged. When administrators proudly tell me how caring their teachers are, I am apt to reply, "That's great. But do you have awards assemblies?" If things have been set up so that one student can succeed only if another fails, if the school sets children against each other in a race for artificially scarce recognition, then nice teachers can accomplish only so much. Similarly, the personal qualities of the staff may not be able to mitigate the harm of practices like posting lists of consequences on the wall or singling children out for public praise. While it's important that the teacher is sympathetic, this does not a community make.

The questions we ought to be asking, in other words, go well beyond "Does this teacher want the best for her students?" We need to ask as well: How does the classroom system work (Alschuler 1980; Bowers and Flinders 1990)? Are students helped to develop a sense of responsibility for each other? By what means? What happens if a child is reduced to tears by cruel taunts, or by deliberate exclusion? What expectations, norms, and structures have been established to deal with such an incident—and to make it less likely to happen in the first place?

Here's a paradoxical exercise worth trying out at a faculty meeting: Start by talking about the meaning of community in a school context. Invite participants to come up with some concrete markers for the concept, some indications of what an observer would see and hear and feel in a place that truly deserved to be called a community. Then ask everyone to think of the most effective ways by which a community can be *destroyed*. If, for some perverse reason, we were determined to eliminate that sense of community, what practices would be most likely to have that effect?

Don't be surprised if participants nominate competition as the number one community destroyer—not only awards assemblies but spelling bees, charts that rank students against each other, grading on a curve, and other things that teach each person to regard everyone else as obstacles to his or her own success (Kohn 1992).

Certain broader educational practices are likely to be mentioned, too. It would be hard to think of a more effective way to snuff out a sense of community than grouping students by putative ability. The most extreme versions of this practice—segregation of students with special needs or of those lucky enough to be deemed "gifted" (Sapon-Shevin 1994)—are likely to have the most extreme effects.

Finally, traditional discipline, or some aspect thereof, may round out the list. That's another reason that this emphasis on community is more controversial than it first appears. (It also explains what a chapter on this topic is doing in a book with a critical perspective on discipline.) The creation of caring communities clashes with the theory and practice of classroom management. It's not just that students who truly feel part of a community are less likely to do the things that bring down the weight of discipline on their heads. It's that a serious commitment to building community offers an invitation to move beyond discipline.

# PSEUDOCOMMUNITY

Talk about turning classrooms and schools into communities may make some people nervous for another, very basic reason: anything that smacks of a social orientation can raise suspicions in a culture like that of the United States. Some see any emphasis on community as a potential threat to the rights of the individual.

Is there reason to be concerned? It is certainly true that some sort of balance needs to be struck between the rights or needs of the group and those of each person in the group. But the United States in general, and U.S. schools in particular, are tilted so far toward an individualist ethic that we have a long way to go before we have to worry about excess in the opposite direction. (This may not be true in places like Japan.) Here, students are given solitary seatwork assignments followed by solitary homework assignments followed by solitary tests. At best, they are exhorted to take responsibility only for their own behavior.

But we can go further than that. The individual is not likely to be swallowed up in a true community because a community is quite different from a collective. This distinction, vividly drawn by the philosopher Martin Buber, is as relevant to education as to political theory. A community not only preserves and nourishes the individuals who compose it but also underscores the relationships among these individuals. These functions are missing in a collective, whose members must simply overcome their private preferences in order to serve the group. (Interestingly, the latter model calls to mind the emphasis on obedience and loyalty to the social order that defines the work of conservative proponents of character education.)

The distinction between a community and a collective may seem awfully abstract, but it springs to life in real classrooms. There are some places where children develop a genuine commitment to each other and to the "us" composed of these real people. There are other places where children are exhorted to silence their own needs in the name of an abstraction called "the group" or "others"[2]—or are roused to jingoistic fervor in the name of something called "school spirit." The point in a collective is conformity, which pretty well excludes the conflict that is essential from a constructivist perspective (see Chapter 5). "Real community is forged out of struggle," observes one educator. "Students won't always agree on issues, and the fights, arguments, tears, and anger are the crucible from which a real community grows" (Christensen 1994, p. 14).

It may help to think of conformity to a collective as a sort of "pseudocommunity," analogous to what I have called pseudochoice. This is what critics sometimes have in mind when they warn about the dangers of community, which means their criticism might be misplaced. A second version of pseudocommunity is peer pressure. It is discouraging to find thoughtful educators endorsing an arrangement whereby students are essentially bullied by their peers into doing the right thing. Because the pressure comes from other students rather than from an adult, some people confuse this behavior with the dynamics of community. Of course, it is nothing of the kind. The goal is compliance (rather than learning), the focus is on behavior (rather than the students' underlying motives and values), and the climate of the class is characterized by the very opposite of safety, warmth, and trust.

One more variant of pseudocommunity might be identified before we move on to some thoughts about how to establish the real thing. I remember participating in a teacher workshop one summer that featured a rather self-conscious bit of community-building. The participants were divided into colors, and I watched the members of the red group try to carry out their assignment, which was to invent a logo and a slogan. This activity was supposed to model the process of creating "commonality," and these teachers would presumably go back and do something similar with their students.

But why *should* any of these strangers have felt part of the group to which they were assigned? They didn't know each other yet, and there was nothing of substance—no honest commonality—around which to create community. The earnest attempt to get consensus about whether they would henceforth be known as the Red Hot Chili Peppers led me to wonder why anyone should care. Indeed, the participants were not particularly responsive during the exercise, leading the facilitator to assume they were just shy or tired and in need of some artificial inducement to participate more energetically. But the problem was not with the attitudes of the individuals; it was with the forced attempt to create a community out of thin air.

## BUILDING A COMMUNITY: PREREQUISITES

A real or authentic community doesn't feel empty. It is constructed over time by people with a common purpose who come to know and trust each other. Of course, it is precisely the commitment to make a community that helps these things happen. But a bunch of strangers cannot be tossed into a room and expected to emerge in a matter of hours as anything more than a bunch of acquaintances.

If the strangers are students and the room is in a school, there are three essential prerequisites for helping them build a community. First, they need time. A schedule that limits them to 45 minutes a day together, like "pull-out" programs that regularly remove some of their members, makes it much harder to succeed. By contrast, the chance for a teacher to work with the same group of students for more than one year makes it easier to succeed (Burke 1996).

Second, they need to be relatively few in number. Lost in the debate about whether excessive class size interferes with academic achievement is its unequivocal effect on a sense of community. Things become even more problematic when the whole school is too large (see Meier 1995).

Finally, they need a teacher who is herself part of a community of adults in the school. Just as teachers who are controlled from above tend to control those below, so teachers who are not part of a collaborative network of educators find it difficult to help students work together. What's more, research has found that shallow, unimaginative instruction—as well as a cynical set of beliefs about children—tends to be associated with teachers who are left to their own devices and wind up valuing their privacy more than anything else. To put this positively, teachers who do exemplary work in helping students engage deeply with what they are learning are invariably part of collegial communities of educators (McLaughlin 1993).

Where those communities do exist, teachers always seem to be in and out of each other's rooms—not as part of a formal (and intimidating) observation process but in order to give and receive feedback voluntarily. Teachers feel safe enough to acknowledge they need help with a problem instead of pretending they have everything under control. They have frequent opportunities to discuss their work—general pedagogical issues or the status of a particular student—with their colleagues. A real effort is made to address threats to community such as cliques or rivalry between teachers. Besides improving the quality of life for the educators themselves, such a school provides the skills and support that will help them replicate this community in their own classrooms.

## BUILDING A COMMUNITY: STRATEGIES

Someone more interested in constructing a community than destroying it might well begin by thinking about how to promote a feeling of *safety*. What can be done in a classroom or school to help every student feel at ease? What can be done to minimize the chance of being ridiculed—by children or adults?

As is so often the case, the best way to proceed is to ask the students these very questions. Early in the year, a teacher might say, "Look, it's really important to me that you feel free to say things, to come up with ideas that may sound weird, to make mistakes—and not to be afraid that other people are going to laugh at you. In fact, I want everyone in here to feel that way. What do you think we can do to make sure that happens?" (Notice that this is another example of meaningful student choice within a teacher-devised framework.)

The ideas that students come up with, perhaps after a few moments of quiet reflection or conversation with a partner, ought to be written down, discussed, and posted. They also ought to be amended later, as needed, when new situations present themselves. For example, imagine that the teacher asks a question of the whole class one morning, and someone waves his hand while exclaiming with boastful disdain, "That's easy!" It might occur to another student that this is a perfect example of how *not* to foster safety or trust. Without humiliating the first student, the teacher might ask everyone to think about how it feels to hear someone else say that a question you are struggling with is supposed to be easy to answer. (Of course, the teacher may need to consider that the underlying problem rests with the whole instructional model that calls for students to race to answer factual questions posed by the teacher.)

The pursuit of safety in particular, or community more generally, is a project best pursued on four levels at once: strengthening the adult's relationship with each student; building students' connections with each other, one dyad at a time; providing for numerous classwide and schoolwide activities in which students work together toward a common end; and weaving the goal of community through academic instruction. Let us take each in turn.

**Relationship with the adults.** Children are more likely to be respectful when important adults in their lives respect *them*. They are more likely to care about others if they know *they* are cared about. If their emotional needs are met, they have the luxury of being able to meet other people's needs—rather than spending their lives preoccupied with themselves.

To be a *caring* person, though, an educator must first be a person. Many of us are inclined instead to hide behind the mannerisms of a constantly competent, smoothly controlling, crisply authoritative Teacher (or Principal). To do so is to play a role, and even if the script calls for nurturance, this is not the same as being fully human with children. A real person sometimes gets flustered or distracted or

111

tired, says things without thinking and later regrets them, maintains interests outside of teaching and doesn't mind discussing them. Also, a real person avoids distancing maneuvers such as referring to him- or herself in the third person (as in: "Mr. Kohn has a special surprise for you today, boys and girls").

Here, again, what initially looks like a commonsense prescription reveals itself as challenging and even controversial. To be a person in front of kids is to be vulnerable, and vulnerability is not an easy posture for adults who themselves had to strike a self-protective pose when they were growing up. Moreover, to reach out to children and develop genuine, warm relationships with them may compromise one's ability to control them. Much of what is wrong with our schools can be traced back to the fact that when these two objectives clash, connection frequently gives way to control.

Beyond being a real person, what does it mean for an adult to be caring in a school context? It means remembering details about students' lives ("Hey, George! Did your mom end up taking you to the museum over the weekend?"). It means writing notes to students and calling them up and even visiting them at home. It means being available, as time permits, for private conversations about nothing in particular.

Caring teachers converse with students in a distinctive way: they think about how what they say sounds from the students' point of view. They respond authentically and respectfully rather than giving patronizing pats on the head (or otherwise slathering them with "positive reinforcement"). They explain what they are up to and give reasons for their requests. They ask students what *they* think, and then care about the answers.

Once again, behaviors are less important than the purposes to which they are put. Rule enforcers may indeed be observant—they may, in fact, "continually monitor the class" (Canter and Canter 1992, p. 147)—but not out of any real concern for who their students are and what they need. The vigilance is more about "withitness" (see p. 55) than connection. Similarly, in an article entitled "Prepare to Take Effective Control," teachers are advised "to learn as many names as possible. Your discipline will be far more effective when you can issue a quiet rebuke to a pupil by name" (Wilson 1995, p. A6). The question is not whether a teacher watches or knows his students, but why.

Educators who form truly caring relationships with students are not only meeting emotional needs; they are also setting a powerful example. Whenever an adult listens patiently, or shows concern for someone he doesn't know, or apologizes for something he regrets having said, he is modeling for students, teaching them how they might be with each other.

**Connections between students.** Many elementary school teachers like to have children create their personal "shields," decorated with words or icons that say something about who each child is. But why should students draw their own shields when they could pair up and draw their partners'? From this simple exercise, every student might learn about someone else, disclose something about herself, and figure out how to represent the information about the other child to his satisfaction. In fact, any number of familiar activities, which subtly perpetuate an ideology of independence, could be transformed into a lesson in *inter*dependence.

In some classrooms, students experience cooperation only when the teacher announces that it is time for cooperative learning. This is not enough, however: communities are built upon a foundation of cooperating throughout the day, with students continually being invited to work, play, and reflect with someone else. Of course, solitary activity has its place, too, but doing things together ought to be, as a computer programmer might put it, the "default setting" in class. Students should have the chance to interact with virtually every other student at some point. This can include getting-to-know-you activities (for example, interviewing someone and then introducing him or her to the class) as well as periodic opportunities to find a partner and check in about whatever is being discussed at the moment.

A community rests on the knowledge of, and connections among, the individuals who are part of it. This knowledge, in turn, is deepened by helping students imagine how things appear from other people's points of view. What psychologists call "perspective taking" plays a critical role in helping children become generous, caring people (Kohn 1990a), and activities designed to promote an understanding of how others think and feel (Feshbach et al. 1983) have the added advantage of creating the basis for community.

**Classwide and schoolwide activities.** While it is important to cultivate the teacher's relationship with each student, and each student's relationship with others, the recipe for community also calls for plenty of opportunity for the whole class to collaborate on common endeavors. Thus, a teacher might have all her students work together to produce a class mural, or collage, or quilt; to choose or even compose a class song; to decide on a name or image that captures the spirit of the class[3]; to write a book, stage a play, or publish a newspaper together; or to do some community service activity as a class (see Child Development Project 1996a, pp. 20–23).

The single most significant and multifaceted activity for the class as a whole is the class meeting, described at length in the previous chapter. Such a meeting at the beginning of the year can be particularly effective at helping students experience themselves as part of a community. Rather than asking students to simply create a list of rules, though—or worse, getting them to think up consequences for individuals who break the rules—the teacher might propose some broader questions for discussion: "What makes school awful sometimes? Try to remember an experience during a previous year when you hated school, when you felt bad about yourself, or about everyone else, and you couldn't wait for it to be over. What exactly was going on when you were feeling that way? How was the class set up?"

Not enough teachers encourage this sort of rumination. Particularly in elementary schools, one often finds an aggressively sunny outlook, such that space is made only for happy feelings. (In a 3rd grade classroom in Minnesota, I once saw a poster near the door that read: ONLY POSITIVE ATTITUDES ALLOWED BEYOND THIS POINT. The message here might be restated as "Have a nice day—or else.") Alas, feelings of anger or self-doubt do not vanish when their expression is forbidden.

We can put such feelings to good use by inviting students to consider carefully why some of their previous school experiences provoked negative reactions. And, of course, the crucial follow-up question is this: "What can we do this year to make sure things go better?" It may make sense to ask students to recall some good memories, too—memories of when school was exciting and appealing, and real learning was taking place—and then puzzle out the common denominators of *those* experiences so they might be re-created this year.

Here is a second way to help students think past the confines of discipline—and to use an early class meeting to begin fostering a sense of community.[4] Begin by asking this question (adapting it as necessary to the students' developmental level): "What if, some time this year, you found yourself acting in a way you weren't proud of? Suppose you hurt someone's feelings, or did something even worse. How would you want us, the rest of the community, to help you then?" After everyone has reflected privately on this question, and perhaps discussed it, pose the follow-up question: "What if *someone else* acted that way? How could we help that person?"

This thought experiment represents nothing short of a revolution in thinking about classroom problems. Actions that would normally be defined as misbehavior—and therefore as requiring discipline—are reconstrued as signs that somebody needs help. If a student had trouble with long division, after all, we would naturally want to help him understand the procedure (and its rationale), rather than seeking to punish him. So if a student instead had trouble, say, controlling her temper, our response again ought to be "How can we help?"—not "What consequence should you suffer?" We should ask, in other words, "What can we do for you?"—not "What can we do *to* you?"

It works both ways, really: The best choice for dealing with problems, or for preventing their occurrence in the first place, is to invoke the support and ideas of the community. And the best choice for building a community may be to take on this sort of challenge together.

Now let's take that idea one step further. If activities and discussions involving the whole class can help to turn that class into a community, then activities and discussions involving the whole school might help to turn the entire student body into a community. The fact that few schools have tried schoolwide discussions may suggest that few schools are small enough to allow everyone to gather and do anything other than listen passively. Fortunately, some creative educators are finding ways around the barrier of size. Each solution amounts to a different way of setting up mini-communities within the school.

• An elementary school in Minnesota reserves an afternoon every week for what might be called advisory groups (more commonly found in cutting-edge secondary schools). Each cluster consists of two kindergartners, two 1st graders, and so on—as well as two adults, one of whom is typically a staff member who doesn't teach. (Office assistants, custodians, cafeteria workers, and others are, after all, part of the school community, too.) People spend their time together getting to know each other, learning conflict resolution skills, and doing service projects.

• An elementary school in Florida divides its entire student body into four parts, with each grade represented in proportion to its total numbers—in effect, creating four small schools. Every day begins with a morning meeting for each community.

• A number of schools have begun to pair classrooms of older and younger students—say, a 5th grade with a 1st grade—for a block of time every week or two, with each child assigned a "buddy" from the other class. Wildly popular wherever it is tried, this activity creates focused cross-age interactions that can improve the feel of the whole school.

> When children are given opportunities to develop caring, trusting friendships across grade levels, when these friendships center around shared learning experiences that are engaging for both older and younger students, and when students see that their teachers have buddies, too, the concept of community is experienced, not just idealized (Child Development Project 1996b, p. 1).

The Child Development Project has developed a series of other schoolwide programs toward the same end, many of which involve families. These include a film night (with the movie selected for its potential for generating thoughtful discussion), a science display (in place of the usual science fair, where parents are not supposed to help with the projects and students are forced to compete against each other), and a read-aloud activity (Child Development Project 1994).

**Using academic instruction.** The quest for community is not—indeed, cannot be—separate from what students are learning. Teachers can deliberately use one to promote the other in any of several ways.

First, community-building activities can be devoted to academic issues. If a class meeting can be used to talk about the best way to make sure that materials are put back where they belong, then why can't one be devoted to talking about how to approach the next unit in history—or how confusing last night's homework was? In fact, even when meetings are not explicitly devoted to curricular questions, they often provide intellectual benefits as students learn to think clearly about problems.

Second, skillful teachers can often find a way to work academic lessons into other tasks and discussions. I visited a kindergarten in New Jersey where students had complained about "too many floods in the bathroom." The problem became a science lesson, as the class generated hypotheses about why the floods were happening, and also a lesson in reading and writing, as the teacher helped students record various proposals for solving the problem. In Japanese elementary schools, academic skills are similarly woven through community-building activities (Lewis 1995).

Third, academic study is pursued cooperatively: students learn from each other and, in the process, form connections with each other. Cooperative learning is likely to provide these benefits, however, only if it is not based on incentives—a process I have called "group grade grubbing" (Kohn 1991)—and if teams are never set against each other in a competition.

Finally, elements of the curriculum may be selected with an eye to supporting social and moral growth and, indirectly, the construction of community. This can be done most readily in language arts units, with works of literature chosen and taught in such a way as to promote reflection about things like fairness and compassion, along with topics such as narrative construction and character development.

# ALL OF THE ABOVE

This last example of how academic instruction can support social learning gives us a chance to pull back and reflect on the larger question of how building community may have certain academic prerequisites. Recall that this chapter began with the argument that a classroom devoid of community, one where children's need for connection is thwarted, has an adverse impact on learning. So it is that the absence of a learner-centered curriculum makes it difficult to create a real community:

> How could we create a caring community in the classroom when children's own needs—to make sense of the world, to be known and liked by others, to influence the environment—were being ignored by a skill-and-drill curriculum? A curriculum that holds little intrinsic interest for children forces teachers to use "motivators," "consequences," and competition to keep children on-task, thereby undermining community and demonstrating that some children are more valued than others (Lewis, Schaps, and Watson 1995, p. 552).

Another teacher describes the problem even more bluntly: "I can sit students in a circle, play getting-to-know-you games until the cows come home, but if what I am teaching in the class holds no interest for the students, I'm just holding them hostage until the bell rings" (Christensen 1994, p. 15).

If we are committed to moving beyond discipline, we need an engaging curriculum *and* a caring community. But we need something else as well: the chance for students to make meaningful decisions about their schooling. That, of course, was the subject of the last chapter, but it is worth reiterating here that a community without choices is just as incomplete as choices without community.

This incompleteness is painfully obvious when we visit "schools with a 'community' emphasis where children memorize 'correct' answers to moral questions and issues" (Goodman 1992, pp. 156–157).

It is obvious when we read manuals for teachers filled with practical advice on how to design a safe, caring classroom—except that the students have little to say about how or why this happens: the teacher is essentially advised to *impose* a community, using praise, time-outs, and other mechanisms of control (e.g., Charney 1991).

And let's add one more piece of evidence to the case against such an approach: in the course of its research, the Child Development Project discovered that elementary school students who reported feeling a sense of community in their classrooms were also apt to exhibit *low* levels of moral reasoning if they lacked an active role in decision making. More sophisticated, principled ways of thinking about ethical questions went hand in hand with community only in those classrooms where students were involved in choosing how to design that community (Battistich et al. 1994).

Community is not enough; we need autonomy, too. In fact, when both of these features are present, there is another way to describe the arrangement that results: it is called democracy.

∞

*autonomy = freedom*

# Chapter 8

# SOLVING PROBLEMS TOGETHER

---

[Some teachers tend to] focus on what is happening rather
than on what is being learned. They may wish simply to stop
the incident rather than consider which of many possible
interventions is mostly likely to stimulate long-term
development and learning.

—Lilian Katz, "The Professional Early Childhood Teacher"

∞

## TWO ROADS DIVERGED . . .

No degree of skill or care on the part of an educator can cause all
problems in the classroom to vanish. A teacher can do only so much
when her students come from homes where power is valued more
than reason or love—or when the culture as a whole reflects similar
priorities. Besides, when two or three dozen people spend the day
together, there are bound to be conflicting needs and clashes of will
that occasionally get out of hand. How do we respond in such
cases—and what do we do when a student makes it hard for others
to learn or even to feel safe?

Various answers to these questions have been offered, and this
chapter will provide some more. But as important as it is to know
how to deal with disturbances, the more compelling question is how
we should regard those disturbances in the first place. The lens
through which we view what students do helps to determine how

useful our reactions will be. To have a constructive impact, in other words, it may be necessary not merely to treat children differently, but to *see* them differently.

Suppose a student does something hurtful or mean. Immediately we make a choice about how to construe what has happened and what ought to be done.

Option 1: "He has done something bad; now something bad must be done to him."

Option 2: "We have a problem here; how are we going to solve it together?"

The first response is so familiar to us that we sometimes lose sight of the fact that it isn't the only possibility. (Recall the popular dichotomy described in Chapter 3: either we punish or we do nothing at all.) What's more, even if we do realize that the first choice isn't the only one, it can be hard to abandon something that keeps us comfortably in control.

The second way of viewing misbehavior is animated not so much by an idealistic vision as by rock-bottom pragmatism. That option represents the only hope of significantly reducing the recurrence of such behavior over the long haul, and the only hope of helping children grow into decent adults. We may not know exactly what to do when kids are disruptive or disrespectful or otherwise disagreeable, but in order to do any good, our point of departure should always be this: *How can we work with students to solve this problem? How can we turn this into a chance to help them learn?*

When a student has done something truly offensive or even dangerous, thinking in these terms is more challenging. But that doesn't mean we should react in the conventional way; it just means that we should try harder than ever to resist that impulse. It takes courage not to punish and, as Lilian Katz observes at the beginning of this chapter, it takes effort to look at misbehavior as an opportunity to teach.

# TEN SUGGESTIONS

Agreeing that we should think in problem-solving terms is one thing; figuring out how to solve real problems in real classrooms is another.

The temptation is to turn to books or workshops that offer recipes—that is, specific prescriptions for what to do, how to talk, even where to stand, when students do something objectionable. But there is reason to be deeply suspicious of this kind of advice. It's disrespectful to teachers when someone proposes to replace their judgment with a packaged response. Moreover, prefabricated interventions are rarely useful for getting to the bottom of problems since they usually turn out to be ways of punishing or otherwise controlling students.

The infinite number of possible problems, not to mention all the circumstances in which they can occur, make it impossible for a responsible author or consultant to offer anything more than general guidelines or considerations to keep in mind. This means, among other things, that *there isn't "an alternative" to traditional discipline.* The number of alternatives is unlimited—though all the legitimate ones can be classified as ways of solving problems and teaching.

Some teachers reply that this approach is "impractical" or "unrealistic" or "nice in theory, but . . ." They say they've *tried* talking to students—in fact, they've talked until they're blue in the face, and nothing ever seems to change. As I see it, this is roughly analogous to saying, "I've been sitting at my word processor for months, typing like mad, and I still haven't produced a good novel. Obviously *typing doesn't work.*"

Of course, the trouble isn't with the technique of typing, per se. Likewise, a "working with" approach shouldn't be abandoned if it fails to produce satisfactory results immediately. (This is especially true in light of the fact that it must be weighed against "doing to" tactics, all of which tend to fail in the long run.) When one approach to solving problems doesn't work, the sensible thing to do is modify the approach. The following suggestions are intended as possible explanations for what may have gone wrong, as well as ideas for becoming more effective next time.

1. It's hard to work with a student to solve a problem unless the two of you already have a **relationship** on which to build. As a general rule, it's important for students to trust their teacher, to know she respects them and to feel safe in speaking their minds with her. But nowhere is such a relationship more vital than in the case of a

student who has done something wrong and feels angry or defensive. Just as a class meeting is most likely to resolve conflicts if a sense of community has been established, so a private conference is most likely to be productive if the student feels accepted by the adult. No problem-solving strategy, regardless of how clever or well-meaning it may be, can take the place of that experience of being accepted.

At the same time, conversations with students when things go wrong can be used to reassure them of the trust and caring that already exist; they can strengthen the bond that is necessary to work things out. For example, a teacher can express strong disapproval of what that student has done to a peer, but add, "I would never let anyone do something like that to you" (Katz 1984). This response accomplishes several things at once: it distinguishes between the act and the actor, leaving no doubt that the student is still cared about and still has rights; and it communicates that the act is unacceptable because of its effect on the victim, not because the teacher happens not to like it, or because it breaks a rule.

If that victim is the teacher himself, the same principles apply. If a student says something nasty about him, or shouts an obscenity at him, it makes sense for him to be honest about how hurt or angry that makes him feel. The teacher is not reacting as an authority figure trying to stamp out a behavior and regain control, but simply as one human being in relation to another.

2. If a caring relationship with each student is a prerequisite for solving problems or resolving conflicts effectively, it is not the only one. Also required is a certain set of **skills**. The teacher may need to help students learn to listen carefully, calm themselves, generate suggestions, imagine someone else's point of view, and so on. Ideally, children should have the chance to work on these skills from the time they are very young. Like us, they need guidance and practice to get better. And it's important to keep in mind that if a student seems unresponsive when asked to take some responsibility for undoing the damage he did, the reason may have less to do with his attitude than with his lack of experience in figuring out what to do.

3. The adult's role in dealing with an unpleasant situation begins with the need to **diagnose** what has happened and why. Punish-

ments and rewards are unproductive in part because they ignore the underlying reasons for a given behavior. If you have a relationship with a child built on trust and respect, you can gently ask her to speculate about why she hurt someone else's feelings, or why she keeps coming to class late. For a variety of reasons, however, such prompting may not be enough, and you will sometimes need to play detective and try to figure out what is going on—or how to interpret what the child is telling you.

I happened to be observing in a kindergarten in eastern Pennsylvania one morning when two children who seemed to spend a lot of time together got into a fight. One started kicking the other. The teacher, a warm, caring woman, immediately took them aside and asked what had happened. But she seemed not to catch the import of their halting accounts, which was that one child misinterpreted the playful intent of the other's horseplay and retaliated in earnest. (Indeed, it can be difficult for children of that age to think in terms of intent at all.)

Because she didn't really understand why the fight had started, how a playful shove was misread as a sign of anger, she wasn't able to offer much of value to help the children head off future conflicts. All she left them with was a rather hollow piece of advice: "Don't kick if someone is lying on the floor; you need to talk."*

4. To figure out what is really going on, we must be willing to look beyond the concrete situation in front of us. This is not easy to do when our patience is frayed, or when there is an urgent need to take some sort of action. It is even more difficult to consider causes and contexts when that process raises **questions about our own practices**. But a real solution to classroom problems often requires that we do just that.

Consider a student who repeatedly shows up late. The traditional response is to threaten zeroes, detentions, and other punishments to

---

*Of course, the teacher might have attributed a fixed characteristic ("aggressiveness") to one of the children, or tried to teach a lesson to one or both of them by imposing a time out or other punishment. That way, she not only would have failed to solve the underlying problem but would have made things much worse to boot.

coerce him into promptness. The "alternative," some educators assert, is to sit down with the student and work it out: get him to take responsibility for changing his behavior.

But is that really the only other option? *Both* of these approaches identify the student as the sole source of the problem and conveniently let us off the hook. It may be necessary to ask ourselves (or him, or the class) what's really going on here. Is the student angry at us? If so, is it for legitimate reasons? Is he angry about something outside of school? If so, can we help? Is he coming to class late because that's as close as he can get to not coming at all? If so, is there something about the class that he finds aversive? What can be done about this? Are other students acting out in different ways that suggest a common pattern?

To take another example, how do we react if a student isn't doing the assigned homework? The worst response—in terms of the likely effects on her attitude toward us, toward herself, and toward the subject matter—is to bully her into turning something in. The more enlightened alternative is to sit down with her and, in a friendly way, get her to come up with a plan that will result in more homework being done.

But again, that is not the only alternative, and it isn't even all that different from the first approach. Neither asks the key question: *What's the homework?* Is it worth doing? How involved were the students in designing it? This line of inquiry takes us beyond the reach of classroom management—which is exactly the point.

5. I have already argued for expanding the role that students play in making decisions. One of many reasons this makes sense is that fewer problems are likely to occur in such an environment. But when problems happen anyway, it is just as critical that we **maximize student involvement** in deciding how to resolve them. Our immediate response—to an individual student in a private conference or to a whole class in a meeting—should be, "What do you think we can do to solve this problem?" Once again, involving students is not just a nice thing to do; it's far more likely to lead to a meaningful, lasting solution than having the teacher decide unilaterally what must be done.

If a conversation with a student produces nothing more than frustration, the problem may just be that the adult is doing most of the talking. With tongue partly in cheek, I will now reveal in four words how to become a better educator: *Talk less, ask more.* This suggestion can be taken quite literally in terms of how much you say in a conversation, but it also reflects a general principle of involving students in figuring out what to do when something goes wrong, and in giving them responsibility for implementing a solution.

In Chapter 6, I talked about how this approach might work with a whole class in preparing for a substitute teacher. Another example, this one involving the entire student body, comes from an elementary school in western Pennsylvania. The problem was how students were behaving in the cafeteria, but the solution was not to discipline those who acted badly: it was to transform the lunchroom into a restaurant. Students chose a theme and began working in committees to decide how to redesign the physically unappealing room, budget their expenses (which created a natural math lesson), provide entertainment, and manage the operation of the restaurant. "We no longer have a lunchroom discipline problem," reports the school's principal, "but we have achieved far more than that" (McBride 1995, p. 66).

6. Asking students to come up with solutions will not get us very far if they feel obliged to cough up explanations, suggestions, or apologies on demand. The questions we ask them must be open-ended, with students encouraged to explore possibilities, reflect on their own motives, disagree, and, in general, to **construct an authentic solution**. This asks a lot of student and teacher alike—perhaps too much on some occasions. But anything short of this is not real problem solving and is not likely to produce worthwhile results.

In another kindergarten classroom, this one in Illinois, I saw two children get into a shoving match one day while lining up to go to lunch. (We'll set aside the possibility that forcing them to line up was not only unnecessary but an invitation for just such behavior.) The two combatants were dispatched to the Problem Solving Corner, where a teacher's aide began by reminding them that they couldn't go to art class until they worked things out. With this inducement to finish quickly, the children guessed what she wanted them to say, and then said it. Would they push each other again? "No." What should they do if someone pushes them? "Come tell the teacher." They were dismissed.

Equally inadequate is a conversation that amounts to a bargaining session, where the student is offered something he wants if he will agree to act the way the teacher wants (e.g., Charney 1991). Here the goal is getting the student to comply with the teacher's wishes—in effect, by offering a reward—rather than helping him develop a commitment to classroom norms. Haggling takes the place of reflection and meaningful decision making.

7. When a student has done something cruel, our first priority is to help her understand that what she did is wrong, and *why* it is wrong, so that it will not happen again. But neither our concern about the future nor a commitment to avoid punishment means that nothing can be done about the past. We don't need to ignore what the student has done. Instead, she can be assisted in thinking about ways to **make restitution** or reparations. A reasonable follow-up to a destructive action may be to try to restore, replace, repair, clean up, or apologize, as the situation may dictate.

At its best, making amends is not seen "as an isolated event, but part of a larger picture of how people treat each other" (Gossen 1992, p. 55). It is "an invitation, not a demand" (p. 124) because "if a student is required to restitute, the act is only a consequence" (p. 151). Fortunately, students are generally inclined to accept that invitation if the classroom feels safe: "When children are not afraid of being punished, they are willing to come forward and make restitution" (Kamii 1984, p. 11).

8. It is often useful to arrange to **check back later** to see how a plan worked, whether the problem got solved, whether additional or entirely new strategies may now be needed. Alternatively, another conversation may be useful just to allow the child to feel proud of himself for the resolution. Such discussions also encourage reflection on the process and consideration of whether it seemed fair and constructive. It is especially important for students to check back later when they have met as a class to solve a problem.

9. Problem solving requires **flexibility** about logist[ic] as about substance. Sometimes you will need to put off a [situa]tion with a student even though it would be better to [right] away.* Sometimes you will have difficulty getting a stud[ent to talk] openly about what is bothering him and it will make mo[re sense to] drop him a note and invite a written response. Sometimes you will notice a pattern of problems and decide to bring this up at a class meeting rather than holding private discussions with individual students. ("Students are often able to solve problems much better than the teacher, simply because there are more of them" [Nelsen 1987, p. 115].) Sometimes you will reach the end of your rope and have to ask a colleague, a spouse, or a student for ideas. In short, "doing to" responses can be scripted, but "working with" responses often have to be improvised.

10. There may be times when no alternative to a "doing to" intervention comes to mind, when one feels compelled to rely on control. If a student persists in disrupting a class meeting, even after repeated reminders that he isn't being fair to everyone else, the teacher may decide to ask him to leave until he is ready to stop acting that way. Everything possible should be done to **minimize the punitive impact** of such a move; the teacher's tone should be warm and regretful, and she should express confidence that the two of them can eventually solve the problem together.

Still, the student may well experience such an intervention as a punishment, and this reaction will make it harder to repair the relationship, address the underlying issues calmly, and so on. For that reason, control is a last-resort strategy to be used reluctantly and rarely. One high school teacher, who liked to think of herself as refusing to tolerate disrespectful behavior, commented:

---

*Note, however, that the likelihood of being able to respond to incidents at the time they happen is not just a matter of chance; to some extent, it reflects instructional design. A teacher who spends much of the day "on stage" will find it more difficult to talk with students during class than a teacher who usually acts as a facilitator for groups of students who are working more or less independently.

If I just kick kids out of class, I "don't tolerate" their actions, but neither do I educate them or their classmates. And it works about as well as stamping out a few ants. I prepare them for repressive solutions where misbehavior is temporarily contained by an outside authority, not really addressed. Sometimes I am forced to that position, but I try not to be (Christensen 1994, p. 16).

# TANYA'S TANTRUM

Here is another activity for a faculty meeting or staff development session: Ask each participant to find a partner and invent a classroom scenario in which a student does something obnoxious or aggressive or otherwise intrusive. Have them fill in as many details as possible to make their descriptions realistic. Then invite each pair to exchange its scenario with another pair. The bulk of the time is spent trying to work out a response to the problem that other participants have devised.

Short of participating in such an exercise, it may be useful to look at a classroom vignette that has been published elsewhere (Collis and Dalton 1990, pp. 31–33) and think about how the teacher handled it—as well as what other teachers had to say about his actions.

> The children in Steve's Grade 6 are busily working in teams spread around the room. Above the general hum of the classroom come two voices raised in argument from near the video recorder. Turning around from his conference group Steve sees Tanya and Troy, both children renowned for temper outbursts, having a tug'o'war with the video's remote control.
>
> Steve moves quickly across the room. "Tanya, Troy, put the remote down, gently," he orders in a quiet but firm voice.
>
> Troy lets go immediately, leaving the remote in the sole custody of Tanya. She promptly lifts it above her head and hurls it at the wall. As it splinters, she yells, "I hate you, I hate this f——ing place and I hate all the kids in it!" and stares defiantly at Steve.

Steve feels the blood rush to his face and the skin tighten on the back of his neck. His first impulse is to hit back—he is angry. In a strained voice Steve orders Tanya and Troy to sit at the opposite ends of an octagonal table.

"I'm too angry to talk now," says Steve. "Sit here until we all calm down enough to talk sensibly about this!" He then moves back to his conferencing group and takes a few deep breaths.

Five minutes go by before Steve stands up again. He moves around the class, pausing momentarily to give feedback to a group that had been sitting near Tanya and Troy. "Thanks for ignoring Tanya and Troy's behavior. They calmed down really quickly because you ignored them."

Eventually Steve makes his way back to the octagonal table and sits down beside Tanya. He turns to Troy and says, "Troy, go on with your contract job and I'll see you after Tanya and I have had a talk." Troy nods and moves away.

Turning toward Tanya, Steve says, "Before we start talking about this, Tanya, you must understand that I will be contacting your parents about what happened. Remember, one of our class rules is that when equipment like this is broken, parents are called." He draws a little closer to her and says softly, "O.K.?"

Tanya looks away sullenly but nods in resignation.

"Right. Tell me what happened," Steve inquires.

"Nothin'," retorts Tanya, eyes diverted away from Steve.

In a voice just audible to Tanya, Steve asserts, "Well, this is what I saw, Tanya. I saw Troy and you fighting."

"Troy wouldn't let me have a turn and he called me a name," Tanya sidetracks.

"O.K. That's what Troy did and I'll be talking with him in a moment. What did you do?"

There is a brief pause that seems like an age to Steve before Tanya offers, "I broke the remote control."

"What happened then?" Steve inquires softly.

"Then I yelled," says Tanya, now looking Steve in the eyes.

"So we've got two problems. You broke the video's remote control and we can't edit the videotape without it; and you got angry and stopped other people in the class from concentrating on what they were learning—right?"

Tanya nods in assent.

"Let's work on one problem at a time. What can we do about the remote control?" Steve asks.

"I could fix it," Tanya offers.

"That's one idea. Can you think of another?" prompts Steve.

"I could pay for a new one, or take it home for Mom or Dad to fix." The ideas come more quickly.

"Have you any more ideas, Tanya?" Steve adds, after a little pause.

"No," replies Tanya.

"So we have three ideas. You could fix it yourself. You could pay for a new one. Or you could ask your parents to help you fix or replace it," Steve summarizes. "Which of those ideas do you think you'll be able to do?"

"Well, I don't think I could fix it myself," Tanya says, looking at the pieces scattered across the floor. "And I haven't got enough money to buy another one." Tanya pauses and looks down at her toes, avoiding any eye contact with Steve.

"So which idea will work for you?" prompts Steve.

"I could ask Mom and Dad to help me fix it or get another one, I suppose," she answers reluctantly.

"So asking Mom and Dad to help you fix it or replace it will best solve our problem of the broken remote?" Steve inquires.

"Yeah," Tanya replies, a little more confidently.

"Well, you talk to your Mom and Dad tonight and we'll get together tomorrow and see how it went. Remember, I'll be talking to them this afternoon, so they'll be expecting you to talk about what happened today pretty soon after you get home, right?" Steve adds, smiling.

Tanya looks up and smiles faintly. "Right," she affirms.

"O.K. That still leaves the problem of getting angry. Let's leave that till next Thursday and tackle that one when we've got a little more time," Steve smiles.

## RESPONDING TO TANYA'S TANTRUM

I have used this episode a number of times as part of a workshop designed to challenge assumptions about conventional discipline. After reading it aloud, I ask participants to temporarily reserve judgment about how well Steve handled the situation and instead simply concentrate on describing the choices he made. I write down all of these descriptions on a flip chart. Only when we have exhaustively summarized his actions do we get to work second-guessing him.

At least two of his decisions are generally accepted as sensible: (1) He waited until he was calm enough to have a productive conversation and made it clear why he was doing so. (2) When he was ready to begin that conversation, he did so by asking Tanya for her version of what had happened.

Other things Steve did, however, are more likely to generate criticism. For example, (3) he hurried over to the two students as soon as he saw them fighting, and he told them what to do with the remote control. Some people wonder whether this intervention was really necessary—and, indeed, whether it might have lit Tanya's fuse.

Also controversial is (4) Steve's comment about calling Tanya's parents. Here two things are going on: (a) the original rule about notifying parents, which was established before this incident, and (b) the fact (and the way) that Steve reminded Tanya about it now.

These are separable: we might object to a fixed policy but believe it is the right thing to do and say here, or we might accept the value of having such a rule but think that his decision to mention it when he did was tactless and unhelpful.

Many teachers wonder how we can expect a student to reflect on what she has done when the conversation is skewed from the start by the announcement that, no matter what is said, the teacher is going to tell her parents what she did. Others rejoin that the extent to which that announcement is perceived as punitive depends on how the parents are likely to react. And yet, if we don't have that information, should we establish a parental-notification policy in the first place? When *do* parents have a right to know?

An even more significant source of disagreement among people who discuss this incident concerns (5) Steve's decision to talk with Tanya and Troy separately. A conversation about this strategy might run roughly as follows:

*First teacher:* I wish he hadn't done that. This was a disagreement between the two kids that escalated, and the two of them need to problem-solve together.

*Second teacher:* I don't know. It may have started as a disagreement between the two of them, but Tanya is the one who broke the remote and screamed an obscenity. Troy had no part in that. Maybe it did make sense to work with her separately.

*Third teacher:* I agree, but for a different reason. What happened between the two kids was only a symptom. Something deeper is going on with this girl that needs to be addressed. I mean, she's talking about hating all the kids, right?

*First teacher:* Hey, all kids have "something deeper" going on, but they have to learn how to resolve conflicts with the people they have those conflicts with, don't they?

*Fourth teacher:* The point isn't whether this incident involved the two of them. The point is whether they're likely to get anywhere if the teacher talks to both of them at once. He's got to know how they're feeling about each other, and they're not going to be as honest if the other one is sitting right there.

*First teacher:* Then that's exactly what they've got to learn how to do!

*Fifth teacher:* Maybe you're both right. Maybe the answer is to have Steve talk to them separately, and *then* together.

*First teacher:* Or together, and then separately.

*Sixth teacher:* Aren't we all taking for granted that the teacher has to be the key element here? If the kids have been trained at conflict resolution—or if there's another kid who can act as a mediator— maybe he can let them work it out themselves.

*Fourth teacher:* Well, I don't know about that. Doesn't he have to get involved when a kid acts as badly as Tanya did? What kind of message is he sending if he stays out of it?

Related to Steve's decision to separate the students is the fact that he also (6) separated the issues. He distinguished the practical problem (a broken remote control) from the question of how Tanya acted, and he dealt with these one at a time. Specifically, he proposed (a) talking about the practical issue first (rather than the other way around) and (b) waiting some number of days before tackling the other one.

Most teachers approve of the separation in principle, but disapprove of his choice to wait so long ("till next Thursday") before meeting with Tanya again to talk about the other problem. It is common, however, for teachers to be split evenly on which problem should have been discussed first, making for a lively exchange:

*First teacher:* Big mistake. He had an obligation, if only to the other students, to get right to the important issue, which was her outburst. If that's not dealt with immediately, the other students won't feel safe. Fixing the remote can wait.

*Second teacher:* Actually, it can't wait. He said they need the thing to edit their tape.

*First teacher:* Well, maybe he should have dealt with both issues that same day, even if he did need to help her see that they're separate.

*Third teacher:* I agree, but I think the main problem is with his priorities. Steve is telling Tanya that the equipment is more important than she is, that a piece of machinery takes precedence over her feelings. I hope he doesn't actually believe that, but I could sure understand if that's how she read it.

*Fourth teacher:* I don't think that's what he's saying at all. And I don't think you're giving him enough credit. Seems to me he's chosen to get Tanya to solve a problem that's—well—solvable. It's easier to get a resolution here, to get the remote fixed, and she can take some pride in having helped to work that out. Then—

*Fifth teacher:* It's not only easier, but it's less messy, less threatening. Get that out of the way first.

*Fourth teacher:* Right. Then, once she feels a little competent, she can figure out what to do about her temper.

*First teacher:* I'm willing to bet she's had plenty of opportunity to feel competent in this classroom, but she's still got a foul mouth and no self-restraint. That's priority number one.

*Sixth teacher:* I agree it's the top priority, but not for the reason you say. I see the way she's acting as the cause, and the broken equipment as the effect. Common sense says you have to deal with the cause first.

*Seventh teacher:* Can I make a suggestion here? Why doesn't the teacher ask *her* which problem to look at first? Why should we take it for granted that he has to make that decision by himself?

. . . and so it goes. These discussions can easily continue for the better part of an hour without much prompting. I make it a point, just as I have done here, to refrain from inserting my own opinion about which position makes more sense. This uncharacteristic reticence is partly due to the fact that I'm not entirely sure that one viewpoint *is* clearly right. But even if I did favor one over another, the point of the exercise, the point of including it here, and, really, the point of this whole chapter, is not to prescribe a formula for dealing with specific scenarios. Rather, I want to emphasize that *educators ought to be having discussions just like this one on a regular basis.*

This is how teachers and administrators get better at their craft: by looking at real classroom scenarios and inviting each other (and themselves) to rethink their assumptions and practices. Evaluating another teacher's choices—being deliberately critical and picking apart his or her every move—is enormously useful. (Of course, it's easier to be uninhibited if the teacher in question is fictional, or at least unknown to the people in the room.)

## "REMEMBER ME?"

Does it make sense, then, to devote some thought to how we can react most productively when something goes wrong in the classroom? Clearly. This chapter, after all, was written for a reason. But should developing a repertoire of responses be our first priority? I don't believe so. There is also a reason that this chapter appears where it does in the book—in sharp contrast to all the writings devoted exclusively to this topic. There are only so many hours in the day, and more of them should be devoted to creating a classroom where problems are unlikely to occur than to rehearsing responses to those that do occur.

When I was teaching, I wanted to hear what experts had to say about specific scenarios: "What do I do when a kid . . . drops his books again, accidentally on purpose . . . curses me out . . . punches another kid?"—and so on. But I wish I had had the presence of mind to ask instead: "How do I turn my classroom into the kind of place where these things rarely happen? How do I help kids become the kind of people who wouldn't *want* to do stuff like this?" The answers to these questions require us to think about who makes the decisions, about how the classroom feels, about our ultimate goals. To that extent, they can be deeply unsettling.

Not long ago, at a workshop in Minnesota where educators were being asked to reconsider traditional assumptions about education, I saw a 1st grade teacher lean over to a colleague during a break and murmur, "Sometimes it makes me feel insignificant." She waved her hand in the air, as if asking to be recognized. "Remember me?" she said plaintively. "I want to be the teacher!"

The question this woman was bumping up against—*What does it mean to be the teacher?*—is at the heart of this book, just as it lurks between the lines of essays about constructivism, Whole Language, and other subjects. Of course, there is a crucial and exciting role for the teacher to play in a learner-centered, "working with" classroom. But that role feels very different from the one that has long been associated with being a teacher: we are no longer front and center, laying out *our* expectations and taking control.

When a comfortably familiar classroom structure is turned inside-out—when what we are asked to do is not what we were trained to do—then, like that 1st grade teacher, we may feel overwhelmed and cry out for the job we knew. Without question, we need plenty of support to make a change of this magnitude. But with that support, and with a vivid awareness of the *need* to make such a change, we can do it. We can create classrooms and schools where students are members of democratic communities. We can move beyond discipline.

∞

# APPENDIX 1
# TEN QUESTIONS

**Q.** **I don't believe there's just one right way to do things, including discipline. Shouldn't we have many different tools in our toolboxes?**

**A.** It all depends on what you're calling a tool. To be sure, we need a range of strategies for working with students. The trouble is that many techniques of discipline or classroom management are actually implements of control rather than tools to achieve legitimate educational ends.

To say this is to make an argument against relativism. Not all strategies are equally good; in fact, some have no place in a caring classroom community. So if, by "different tools," you mean we should be prepared to solve problems with students in many different ways, I'd agree. But if you mean that we need to know not only how to solve problems but also how to apply punitive consequences, then I can't go along.

**Q.** **I just came across a flier for a discipline program that you don't talk about anywhere in this book, and now I'm starting to wonder whether it's just another one of those "New Disciplines" you criticize.**

**A.** My intention is to offer a critical perspective that can be used for evaluating *any* packaged discipline system—or any specific practice, for that matter. The programs I mention by name are meant to serve only as illustrations. As you investigate a given approach to discipline, you may want to ask the questions around which this book is organized: (1) What's the underlying view of children? (2) Is it taken for granted that we should just change the student's behavior when he fails to comply, or is the possibility raised that the problem may lie with the adult's request, or with the curriculum? (3) Does the program propose interventions that are likely to be experienced as punitive or controlling—and that encourage each student to focus mostly on the consequences of her actions to herself? (4) How real and meaningful are the choices being offered to students? (5) Is the ultimate goal to get mindless obedience, or to help children become responsible, caring people?

**Q.** **It occurred to me as I read your comments about punishment and rewards that *I* was mostly punished and**

**rewarded when I was a kid, yet somehow I turned out just fine. How could that be?**

**A.** It would be presumptuous for someone who doesn't know you to question your premise, which is that you turned out "just fine." Many of us, though, may have occasion to probe delicately at what we sometimes take as an article of faith, namely our own psychological health. Perhaps we are less sure of ourselves than we would like to be, or too full of ourselves; habitually mistrustful or misused in relationships; given to depression or defensiveness. Pop psychology books and TV talk shows draw rather simplistic connections between such characteristics and the way we were treated as children. But it would be equally simplistic to deny that there is any connection, to insist that we are just fine and therefore that whatever our parents and teachers did to us must have worked. How many people, to cite just one example, cannot take satisfaction and pride in their own accomplishments until someone vested with greater authority tells them they did a good job? That is exactly what we would expect of an individual who, as a child, was controlled with expressions of contingent approval.

If this sort of probing of your own mental health is too unsettling, then let's assume for the sake of the argument that there is no doubt about how well you turned out. In that case, the question you might want to ask is whether this is true *because of* or *in spite of* being punished and rewarded by significant adults. My guess, based on the available research, is the latter. If I'm right, and if our goal is to maximize the chance that our own children or students turn out well, it would seem to make sense to choose another way.

**Q. What about punishing adults—or don't you believe in prisons?**

**A.** People are put in prison for any of several reasons: to make them suffer in the hope that this will change their behavior; to make them suffer because we want to exact revenge, even if it has no practical benefit; because they are deemed so dangerous that they must be segregated from the population at large; to rehabilitate them; or to deter others from committing crimes.

This isn't the place to analyze the legitimacy of these five very different justifications. But notice that only one of them, the first one, corresponds to what we call punishment (or the use of "consequences") in a school setting. And the bottom line is that harsh, demeaning treatment typically produces more antisocial activity on the part of adults and children alike.

In any case, an endorsement of imprisonment isn't much of an argument for punishing students. Apart from the obvious differences between children and adults, schools are generally asked to play a role very different from that of the criminal justice system.

**Q. I'm still having a hard time with your reluctance to toss out kids who are preventing everyone else from learning. Doesn't creating a community begin by taking a hard line against those who would disrupt it?**

**A.** As I noted in Chapter 8, there may be extraordinary cases, such as when someone poses an immediate threat to others, that prompt us to tell someone he must temporarily leave the group (or the school). But to call attention to this possibility, to take pride in it, or to make it the cornerstone of our educational policy makes no sense for several reasons.

First, tossing someone out does absolutely nothing to help that individual become more ethical or responsible. In fact, it is likely to make things worse in the long run, and that fact needs to be weighed against any benefit that others might gain from his absence.

Second, we need to ask what kind of example we are setting when we kick out someone for misbehaving. While we may insist that it isn't fair to other students if one person is allowed to act like that, those other students—the ones in whose name we are taking this action—are receiving some disturbing messages: "We don't solve problems; we push them out of the way"; "Everyone is part of this community only conditionally"; and "Once you have enough power, you can make other people act the way you want—or else just make them disappear."

Third, creating and sustaining a democratic community means doing everything possible to work out problems with its members, even though the process may try our patience. The seductive luxury of a policy of exclusion, after all, is what defines private schools: they "can get rid of unwanted kids or troublemaker families . . . and toss aside the 'losers'"—in contrast to public schools, which must commit themselves to "the democratic arts of compromise and tolerance" (Meier 1995, p. 7). The credo of democracy is Robert Frost's declaration that "The best way out is always through." It's not easy to reconcile that motto with one such as "Either do it our way or leave."

One last point. It's useful for us as teachers to consider how features of the classroom for which we are primarily responsible might help to explain why a student does something unpleasant (see Chapter 2). Booting that student allows us to duck those troubling issues by placing all the blame on him. Perhaps we shouldn't be surprised that calls for purging schools of the "bad" kids often go hand in hand with simplistic demands for schools to raise standards (e.g., Shanker 1995). The latter is conspicuous for its failure to look deeply into the theories of learning and motivation that underlie our teaching and to examine the extent to which the curriculum is meaningful and engaging. All we have to do, apparently, is ratchet up the difficulty level while getting rid of students who cause trouble: that's how we beat the Japanese.

**Q.  You talk a lot about giving students choices. But aren't there responsibilities that go along with those choices?**

**A.**  The opportunity to make decisions *is* a responsibility: it means students have an obligation to participate in figuring out how things are going to be done in the classroom rather than leaving everything to the teacher.

Some people who talk about the need for students to "take responsibility" for their choices really mean that students should be made to suffer when things don't work out well. I think it makes more sense in that event for them to be part of a nonpunitive problem-solving process.

Others assert that "responsibilities" must balance "rights," and by this statement they apparently mean that when students don't act the way we want, they should lose the opportunity to choose. I don't see decision making as something granted to children conditionally, a kind of reward for compliance that can be yanked away when they act badly. In fact, I can't imagine a situation in which we would remove the chance for students to learn how to make good choices any more than I can imagine a situation where we would remove the chance for them to learn how to read.

**Q.  What will happen if I dump the stickers and star charts in the trash can tomorrow—or stop using consequences?**

**A.**  Here's one thing that *won't* happen: your students will not leap out of their seats, cheering, "Yay! At last we can develop an intrinsic commitment to good values!"

There are at least three reasons they will not do so. Number one: no one asked their opinion. First rewards and punishments were done to them, then the *abolition* of rewards and punishments was done to them. It would be more than a little ironic if the move from "doing to" to "working with" was itself done *to* students. Even good ideas, as many teachers know from experience with administrators, cannot be forced down people's throats.

Number two: students may have become dependent on extrinsic devices. The more you control people, such as with bribes and threats, the more you feel you have to control them, because they have grown accustomed either to doing what someone else tells them or to rebelling. They have also gotten used to asking, "What will you do to me if I don't follow your rule (or do *for* me if I *do* follow it)?" It takes time and effort to help students construct their own reasons to act responsibly and generously.

Number three: it is necessary but by no means sufficient to get rid of the controls. You also have to provide other things I've talked about in this book: the opportunity to make decisions, the caring and safe community, the valuable curriculum, and the social skills. Without these things, chaos may turn out to be the alternative to control after all.

In short, change, particularly a revolutionary change such as this one, must be made gradually, respectfully, and collaboratively. Students should be brought in on the process from the beginning. That process might start with something as basic as an invitation to reflect on how it feels to be managed and controlled.

**Q. Even if I'm ready to make my classroom more democratic or less coercive, how successful can I be if everyone else in my building is still basically trying to control students?**

**A.** The experts in school reform tell us unequivocally that the best way to make change is at the level of the whole school, if not the whole district. But if your colleagues aren't ready to move in this direction, it still makes sense for you to do what you can on your own. Even if students are plunged back into the likes of Assertive Discipline when they leave you, at least they will have had the experience of making decisions, feeling respected, and being part of a community while they were in your class. That will give them a sense of perspective about whatever comes next: they will know that *things could be otherwise.*

If you doubt that you can make a difference by yourself, think back on your own experiences as a student. Was there a teacher who had an effect on your life in a single year? You can be that teacher.

Still, do everything you can to avoid feeling isolated. Even if the faculty as a whole is unwilling to change, try to find a few like-minded colleagues—or even a single partner—with whom to exchange practical solutions and moral support.

**Q. I'm (usually) managing to resist the temptation to rely on consequences and rewards. But a lot of my kids go home every afternoon and get socked with that approach. The**

**parents are of the "Do what I say, or else" school of thought. It makes me wonder how much impact I can really have. Plus, it creates some sticky situations when the students are getting one message at home and another at school.**

A. If such values as respect, caring, trust, autonomy, and reason are present at home, too, then that makes your job easier. If kids *aren't* getting these values at home, that makes your job more important.

You're quite right that inconsistency creates certain problems, whether between last year's teacher and this year's teacher, or between home and school. But consistency in the abstract is less important than the values themselves. After all, a perfectly consistent application of coercion is hardly in the child's interest.

I recognize this assertion raises troubling philosophical questions about the relative responsibilities of parents and teachers. It also raises practical problems, since we need to be respectful of parents regardless of how their approach differs from our own. The best strategy is to invite parents, gently and respectfully, to consider a different way. Help them to see the long-term effects of punishment and rewards, the practical advantages of nonpunitive problem solving, and the ways that bringing children in on making decisions can help them grow into the kind of people we'd all like them to be.

In the meantime, if a student tells you how his parents do things (for example, "My Dad told me I'm supposed to hit back" or "My Mom gives me a treat when I've been good"), the best you can do is (1) tell him that we do things differently here, (2) explain why, and (3) invite him to reflect on the effects of your approach throughout the year.

Q. **I've been reading this book not only as an educator but also as a mother. Are there any resources consistent with this philosophy available to parents?**

A. I'm sorry to report that relatively few parenting books are about meeting kids' needs and working with them to make decisions and solve problems. Most seem to be full of advice on how to "handle" or "train" children, how to outsmart, punish, and otherwise control them. Some are Dreikurs derivatives, filled with logical consequences, and some are even worse. The exceptions, built on a foundation of respecting children and taking them seriously, include the classic works of Haim Ginott and Thomas Gordon, as well as more recent books by Adele Faber and Elaine Mazlish, and by Barbara Coloroso.

∽

# APPENDIX 2
# ASSERTIVE DISCIPLINE: A GLOSSARY

**be•have**  *v.* obey.

*Example*: "Children are not innately motivated to **behave** in school" (Canter and Canter 1992, p. 7). *Comment*: It might be that Canter is simply revealing a profoundly negative view of children (they are bad until you make them good), or a rigidly behaviorist perspective (all actions are initiated by the external environment). But a more reasonable guess is that the word *behave* in this sentence means "do whatever they are told, however unreasonable or uninteresting." In that case, he is right; in fact, *no one* is "innately motivated" in this sense, nor should anyone be.

**help**  *v.* make, compel.

*Example*: "I have to find a way to **help** you behave more appropriately in class" (p. 230). *Comment*: It is only in the context of the discipline program as a whole that we know how little helping, and how much controlling, is really going on. Notice also in this sentence (1) the focus (as in the previous entry) not on the child but on the child's behavior, which in itself predicts the use of rewards and punishments, and (2) the word *appropriately*. If it occurs to you to ask, ". . . as determined by whom?", you are disqualified from giving workshops on discipline.

**mean•ing•ful**  *adj.* unpleasant, aversive.

*Example*: "No matter what the consequence, it must always be one that will be **meaningful** to the student" (p. 229).

**mo•ti•vat•ed**  *adj.* obedient, compliant.

*Example*: If you single out one student for praise, "other students will get the message that you are aware of what's going on in the room, and will be **motivated**. . . ." (p. 151). *Comment*: You have never met a child who wasn't motivated. You have, however, met plenty of children who weren't motivated to take their seats on command, follow a rule whose rationale they didn't understand, or memorize a bunch of lists. If we had a nickel for every time an educator used the word *motivation* when he or she was really talking about compliance, we could fund inner-city schools at suburban levels.

**re•spect**  *n.*  fear.

*Example:* "In the not-so-distant past . . . children knew that if they got in trouble at school, they'd be in twice as much trouble at home. Consequently, a vast majority of children came to school with built-in **respect** for teachers. . . ." (p. 6)

**re•spon•si•ble**  *adj.*  obedient, compliant. See Motivated.

*Example:* "CHAPTER 9: TEACHING **RESPONSIBLE** BEHAVIOR. . . . Highly successful teachers . . . take time to teach their students exactly how they want them to behave in all classroom situations . . . until all students know *how* to line up for recess, *how* to go to learning groups, and *how* to return to class after lunch" (pp. 121–122; emphasis in original). *Comment:* This usage, of course, has been around long before Assertive Discipline. William Glasser (1969, p. 22) observed years ago that "we teach thoughtless conformity to school rules and call the conforming child 'responsible' " — and John Holt said much the same thing even earlier. For that matter, I once worked in a school where the principal frequently exhorted students to "take responsibility." What he meant was that they should turn in their friends who used drugs.

∞

# NOTES

## Notes to Chapter 1: The Nature of Children

1. The behaviorist "view of the child as originally an empty organism who learns to incorporate behaviors on the basis of external rewards or punishments . . . seems a neutral view of the child, but the underlying assumption is that all are striving to maximize their self interest. Thus, we end up with a view of children as primarily selfish, and subject to control only by the application of rewards and punishments" (Watson 1984, p. 36; also see Kohn 1990a).

2. These theories concerning the psychological significance of being the first-born or youngest child are repeated uncritically by Dreikurs (Dreikurs et al. 1982, chap. 7) and the author of a program called Positive Discipline (Nelsen 1987, chap. 3). Unfortunately, rigorous scientific research has repeatedly failed to support almost all claims related to birth order. (For a brief review, see Kohn 1990b, pp. 144–148.)

3. Otherwise, in the words of two students of Dreikurs, one only "reinforces [an] inappropriate desire for attention" (Dinkmeyer and McKay 1989, p. 10). This tendency to cite (in dismissive tones) a "need for attention" as the reason a child has done something seems to assume, as one writer put it, that "wanting to be noticed [is] a mysterious or stupid need" (Lovett 1985, p. 69). It's rather as though someone were to say about an adult, "Oh, well, she only goes out to dinner with friends because of her 'need for companionship.'"

4. Apart from casting children in the worst possible light, this is one of several assertions made by Dreikurs that seem difficult to substantiate, if not downright perplexing. He declared at another point that children with poor handwriting, or problems with spelling, typically have "little respect for order" (Dreikurs et al. 1982, p. 205; Dreikurs and Cassel 1972, p. 90). And he complained about how difficult it is to stop "parents, particularly mothers, from talking incessantly," adding that "fathers usually do not talk as much and, therefore, the children listen to them" (Dreikurs et al. 1982, pp. 339–340).

5. Marilyn Watson, personal communication, 1995. Watson is the program director of the Child Development Project in California, which I discuss in a later chapter.

6. Three of the four basic needs proposed by William Glasser (1986) correspond to this framework: freedom (autonomy), love (relatedness), and power (competence). Glasser suggests a need for fun as well.

## Notes to Chapter 2: Blaming the Kids

1. Or perhaps she had just been trained in Assertive Discipline, which suggests that a 4th, 5th, or 6th grade teacher announce to the class, "If you need to get a sharpened pencil, raise your dull pencil in the

air. When I give you permission, you may place your pencil in the 'dull' pencil cup and take a sharpened pencil from the cup marked 'sharpened.' Then return immediately to your seat and begin working" (Canter and Canter 1992, p. 136).

2. We should be quite familiar with this euphemism—and wary about using it on students—in light of how often policymakers brandish it as a way to justify blaming teachers for systemic problems that make learning so difficult. Demands for accountability almost always accompany prescriptions for tighter control—control of what happens in classrooms by people who aren't in them, and control over students by teachers.

3. Actually, the introductory Cooperative Discipline video (Albert 1992b) does contain one attempt to demonstrate that children's misbehavior is something they "choose": the program's developer asks her audience to recall how, when they were in high school, they acted differently in different classes. "What changed from one period to another?" she asks, to which someone replies, reasonably enough, that each class had a different teacher. But this is not the answer she is looking for, so it is brushed aside in favor of the view that *they* (the students) changed—ergo, one's behavior is freely chosen. (A very similar "proof" is offered in Assertive Discipline [Canter and Canter 1992, p. 21].)

4. Interestingly, the research in question was conducted by behaviorists. The larger point that discipline problems are related to the value (not merely the difficulty) of the curriculum was made decades ago by John Dewey. And a few others outside the field of classroom management have taken up the cry: "If school is not inviting, if the tasks are not clear, interesting, and at an appropriate level, how can we expect pupils to be on task? Adverse student reactions should be expected when classes are dull, teaching is uninspired, and failure is built in. Their oppositional behavior is a sign of personal health and integrity" (Morse 1987, p. 6).

## Notes to Chapter 3: Bribes and Threats

1. Perhaps staying after school is not unpleasant to a child who is in no hurry to go home, or an F means little to a student who is not preoccupied with grades, or a public criticism intended to elicit shame produces only amusement. Even paddling can expiate guilt. Any number of frowning psychologists and educators have expressed their concern about poorly chosen punishments and the need to implement the concept more carefully—which means, in such a way that the child will really suffer. I question the value of the concept itself.

2. Negligence by parents is another likely explanation for children who grow up to act in disturbing ways, but insufficient attention or nurturing is all too compatible with punishment and control. There may

be some disagreement about whether aggressive children are more likely to come from families that are (a) chaotic, (b) punitive, or (c) both, but it is hard to dispute that such children almost never come from families where adults work with children respectfully to solve problems.

3. The research substantiating the detrimental effects of punishment has been accumulating for decades. Among the most influential investigators in the field are Martin Hoffman, Diana Baumrind, and Robert Sears. Some citations to their work, as well as to more recent studies, appear in Kohn 1993a; see esp. pp. 165–168 and 329–330$n$25.

4. And: "The more you want to teach children how to behave, the more you need to use praise" (Canter and Canter 1992, p. 145). If this is true, it may be an invitation to question the traditional, autocratic assumptions built into the word *teach* in that sentence.

### Notes to Chapter 4: Punishment Lite

1. This impression is corroborated by the fact that Lee Canter's short list of "Additional Readings in Behavior Management" includes some of the very approaches that are thought to offer something different: Rudolf Dreikurs, Linda Albert's *Cooperative Discipline,* and another Dreikurs derivative called the "STEP" program.

2. Earlier in this same book, teachers are urged to "reinforce positive behavior" (Dreikurs et al. 1982, p. 36)—and elsewhere, to "praise [a child] when her behaviour is acceptable" (Dreikurs and Cassel 1972, p. 93). He also uses as an example of "encouragement" the sort of response that most of us would consider traditional praise: "I like your drawing. The colours are so pretty together" (p. 56).

3. Discipline with Dignity does improve on Assertive Discipline in one respect, at least, by urging that children should be praised in private. But the chapter in which this advice appears could have been lifted, with very few modifications, straight from Canter's book: its specific suggestions for implementing consequences (be consistent, don't accept excuses, ignore students when they argue with you, speak firmly but calmly, etc.) closely follow the Assertive Discipline approach to behavior management. The exhortation to "catch students being good" is difficult to reconcile with some pointedly critical remarks about praise offered some pages before (Curwin and Mendler 1988, pp. 84–86)—but then again, this earlier section is oddly inconsistent in its own right: we are told that praise "can be highly manipulative" in that the teacher is "really saying, 'You can have my approval only by doing what I decide is right for you'" (p. 84), but two pages later, a list of characteristics of "effective praise" (uncritically appropriated from another writer) begins by urging teachers to ensure that praise is delivered "conti[n]gently" (p. 86).

4. The clipboard is supposed to represent an important improvement over the first version of the program, which recommended posting

names on the blackboard. In the revised edition of his book, Canter noted that "unfortunately, some individuals have misinterpreted the use of names and checks on the board as a way of humiliating students" (Canter and Canter 1992, p. 90)—as if the fault rested with the people who implemented this technique rather than with the technique itself. Incidentally, a recent report from England, where Canter has licensed a training program in Assertive Discipline only since 1990, suggests that names are still being written on the blackboard there (Dore 1994).

5. This estimate almost certainly understates the actual prevalence of abuse since it is based exclusively on parents' own reports—that is, what they admitted to Gallup pollsters. Moreover, "abuse" was defined so as to exclude more common forms of violence against children, such as slapping or spanking. Verbal abuse and other forms of punishment also were not counted.

6. Dreikurs's solution is to put two books under the front legs of the chair, forcing the student to lean back in a way that is deliberately uncomfortable "until he decide[s] to sit properly" (Dreikurs and Grey 1968, pp. 78–79).

7. Ironically, we can do no better than take Dreikurs's own dictum seriously: "The most important element . . . [is] *How* does *the child* view the situation?" (Dreikurs and Grey 1968, p. 81; emphasis in original).

8. For other examples in which Dreikurs advises a teacher to talk about a child in front of his peers or, in effect, make those peers her accomplices against him, see Dreikurs et al. 1982, pp. 39, 166.

9. While this suggestion would seem to be only common sense, even for teachers who favor the practice, one writer explicitly recommends using time-outs for every minor behavior that the teacher deems unacceptable. All a child has to do is interrupt someone or continue to work at an activity after a signal to stop, and he or she should be forced to leave the group. The rationale offered for this tactic is that it will stop small problems before they become "explosions" (Charney 1991, pp. 94, 99). Proponents of frequent time-outs assume not only that a constant flow of punitive interventions will create a peaceful classroom, but also that the *only* alternative to an explosive situation is to single out children in front of their peers and make them sit by themselves.

10. Offering only two possible courses of action may sometimes be appropriate for very young children, for example. In fact, there are times when the number of options may have to be limited for all students. But it is vital for children to have the opportunity to invent possibilities rather than just selecting from a predetermined menu—much less a menu containing only two entrees. The question becomes where to draw the line, how much to limit choices and when. More about this later.

11. Likewise, "I see you have decided to go to your room" appears in a program called Positive Discipline (Nelsen 1987, p. 164), but this example reportedly will not appear in a forthcoming revision of that book.

## Notes to Chapter 5: How Not to Get Control of the Classroom

1. In the book itself, Phelan suggests that "instead of thinking of your kids as little adults, think of yourself as a Wild Animal Trainer. . . . Choose a method—which is largely nonverbal—and repeat it until the 'trainee' does what you want" (Phelan 1995, p. 12).

2. For what it's worth, Canter told a reporter recently that half of all U.S. teachers have been trained in Assertive Discipline (Dore 1994).

3. All things being equal, kindergartens are more likely to have been designed to promote real understanding and active learning than are classrooms for older students. The National Association for the Education of Young Children, and many individual teachers of preschool through primary grades, are exquisitely attentive to what children need if they are to learn and to love learning. (Not for nothing has Deborah Meier [1995] tried to incorporate aspects of a good kindergarten classroom in formulating a model of a learner-centered high school.) So it is that the best work on fostering sociomoral development—and rejecting the use of traditional discipline—is happening mostly in the field of early childhood education. We can speculate on why this is so, or why "educators in secondary schools have a stronger orientation to control than elementary school educators" (Midgley, Feldlaufer, and Eccles 1988, p. 546), but the more urgent need is to bring the best of that theory, research, and practice to bear on the education of older students, too. While it is an axiom of constructivism that one must attend to developmental differences, the basic values described in this book—active construction of ethical and social meaning; more choices for students; the construction of caring communities; a move away from rewards, punishments, and other tactics of control—both can and should be applied all the way through school (and through life).

4. The very same contrast may be drawn in the case of hurtful actions: on the one hand are what Hoffman calls "power-assertion" techniques that cause the child pain and send a disturbing message ("If you do that again, I will be unhappy—and will make *you* unhappy"); on the other is one person helping another to see how his victim was affected by what he did. In Chapter 1, I cited Marilyn Watson's observation that punitive consequences ("logical" or otherwise) are based on the hidden premise that children will refrain from doing bad things only if we make them suffer. The premise of the inductive approach, by contrast, is that if we help children see how their actions affect others, both positively and negatively, we can generally trust them to want to have a positive impact.

5. One marvels at the lengths to which proponents of this approach will go to deny the obvious: "A stern reminder" that a child has broken a rule "is not a threat that something will happen later, although the assertive tone with which it is delivered should leave no doubt in the student's mind that the next infraction will result in a more active consequence" (Curwin and Mendler 1988, p. 72).

6. This quotation and the following one are taken from personal correspondence from Marilyn Watson (of the Child Development Project) in 1989.

## Notes to Chapter 6: A Classroom of Their Choosing

1. I have discussed the benefits of this kind of choice, as well as some thoughts about how it can be offered, in Kohn 1993b. The following discussion also draws to some extent from the ideas in that article. For a particularly innovative approach by which middle school students can effectively plan their own curriculum, also see Brodhagen 1995.

2. This anecdote first appeared in Kohn 1990c, an article about the Child Development Project, with which this teacher was involved.

3. It is also possible for the teacher to decorate the walls initially but then invite the students to take everything down and redesign the room together.

4. Keith Grove, of Dover-Sherborn High School.

5. The kindergarten teacher, Judy Collier, and the 2nd grade teacher, Terry Anderson, work at Robinson Elementary School in Kirkwood, Mo., near St. Louis.

6. In the words of one Japanese elementary teacher, "Reward children for good behavior? I think it's demeaning. In fact, I wouldn't even want to train animals that way. Even for a dog, it's humiliating to do tricks in the hopes of getting something for it" (quoted in Lewis 1995, p. 124).

7. The unavoidable—and disturbing—implication of this analysis is that very few of us in the United States have ever experienced real democracy. I recommend the work of contemporary political scientists such as Benjamin Barber and Jane Mansbridge for more on how things could be otherwise. Deborah Meier (1995, p. 24) has commented that the "kind of school culture we were trying to create . . . require[d] that most decisions be struggled over and made by those directly responsible for implementing them, not by representative bodies handing down dictates for others to follow."

## Notes to Chapter 7: The Classroom as Community

1. For information about the CDP, or to order the books listed in the reference section under the Child Development Project, write to the Developmental Studies Center, 2000 Embarcadero, Suite 305, Oakland, CA 94606.

2. For that matter, these models even characterize the individual differently. The traditional sensibility that exalts the collective tends to conceive the individual student as an empty receptacle to be filled (with knowledge or values). Those who talk about community likewise acknowledge a tension between an emphasis on us vs. me, but here the "me" is integrally involved in constructing meaning, in being a decision maker whose interests and needs drive the learning. Both the individual and the community are defined by autonomy or self-determination.

3. "In order for a class name to be meaningful, and the process of finding one to be interesting, students need enough information about themselves as a group for the name to reflect the character of the class in some way" (Child Development Project 1996a, p. 63)—and therefore probably should not try to agree on a name during the first week of school.

4. I adapt this teaching strategy from the work of the Child Development Project.

∽

# REFERENCES

Albert, L. (1989). *A Teacher's Guide to Cooperative Discipline: How to Manage Your Classroom and Promote Self-Esteem*. Circle Pines, Minn.: American Guidance Service.

Albert, L. (1992a). *An Administrator's Guide to Cooperative Discipline*. Circle Pines, Minn.: American Guidance Service.

Albert, L. (1992b). *An Introduction to Cooperative Discipline*. Videotape. Circle Pines, Minn.: American Guidance Service.

Albert, L. (September 1995). "Discipline: Is It a Dirty Word?" *Learning*: 43–46.

Alschuler, A. S. (1980). *School Discipline: A Socially Literate Solution*. New York: McGraw-Hill.

Andersen, J. F., and P. A. Andersen. (1987). "Never Smile Until Christmas? Casting Doubt on an Old Myth." *Journal of Thought* 22: 57–61.

Angell, A. V. (1991). "Democratic Climates in Elementary Classrooms: A Review of Theory and Research." *Theory and Research in Social Education* 19: 241–266.

Battistich, V., D. Solomon, D. Kim, M. Watson, and E. Schaps. (1995). "Schools as Communities, Poverty Levels of Student Populations, and Students' Attitudes, Motives, and Performance: A Multilevel Analysis." *American Education Research Journal* 32: 627–658.

Battistich, V., D. Solomon, M. Watson, and E. Schaps. (March 1994). "Students and Teachers in Caring Classroom and School Communities." Paper presented at the annual meeting of the American Educational Research Association, New Orleans.

Battistich, V., M. Watson, D. Solomon, E. Schaps, and J. Solomon. (1989). "The Child Development Project: A Comprehensive Program for the Development of Prosocial Character." In *Moral Behavior and Development: Advances in Theory, Research, and Applications*, edited by W. M. Kurtines and J. L. Gewirtz. Hillsdale, N.J.: Lawrence Erlbaum.

Battistoni, R. M. (1985). *Public Schooling and the Education of Democratic Citizens*. Jackson: University Press of Mississippi.

Berman, S. (1990). "The Real Ropes Course: The Development of Social Consciousness." *ESR Journal*: 1–18.

Bloom, L. A., and M. J. R. Herzog. (1994). "The Democratic Process in Teacher Education: Two Case Studies." In *Democratic Teacher Education*, edited by J. M. Novak. Albany: State University of New York Press.

Bluestein, J. (1988). *21st Century Discipline: Teaching Students Responsibility and Self-Control*. Jefferson City, Mo.: Scholastic.

Blumenfeld, P. C., P. R. Pintrich, and V. L. Hamilton. (1986). "Children's Concepts of Ability, Effort, and Conduct." *American Educational Research Journal* 23: 95–104.

Bowers, C. A., and D. J. Flinders. (1990). *Responsive Teaching: An Ecological Approach to Classroom Patterns of Language, Culture, and Thought*. New York: Teachers College Press.

Brodhagen, B. L. (1995). "The Situation Made Us Special." In *Democratic Schools*, edited by M. W. Apple and J. A. Beane. Alexandria, Va.: ASCD.

Brooks, J. G., and M. G. Brooks. (1993). *In Search of Understanding: The Case for Constructivist Classrooms*. Alexandria, Va.: ASCD.

Burke, D. L. (January 1996). "Multi-Year Teacher/Student Relationships Are a Long-Overdue Arrangement." *Phi Delta Kappan:* 360–361.

Canter, L. (October 1988). "Let the Educator Beware: A Response to Curwin and Mendler." *Educational Leadership:* 71–73.

Canter, L. (Summer 1989). "Assertive Discipline: A Response." *Teachers College Record* 90: 631–638.

Canter, L., and M. Canter. (1992). *Lee Canter's Assertive Discipline: Positive Behavior Management for Today's Classroom*. Santa Monica, Calif.: Lee Canter & Associates.

Center, D. B., S. M. Deitz, and M. E. Kaufman. (1982). "Student Ability, Task Difficulty, and Inappropriate Classroom Behavior." *Behavior Modification* 6: 355–374.

Chanoff, D. (1981). "Democratic Schooling: Means or End? Resolving the Ambiguity." *High School Journal* 64: 170–175.

Charney, R. S. (1992). *Teaching Children to Care: Management in the Responsive Classroom*. Greenfield, Mass.: Northeast Foundation for Children.

Child Development Project. (1991). "Start the Year." Unpublished manuscript. San Ramon, Calif.: Developmental Studies Center.

Child Development Project. (1994). *At Home in Our Schools: A Guide to Schoolwide Activities that Build Community*. Oakland, Calif.: Developmental Studies Center.

Child Development Project. (1996a). *Ways We Want Our Class to Be: Class Meetings that Build Commitment to Kindness and Learning*. Oakland, Calif.: Developmental Studies Center.

Child Development Project. (1996b). *That's My Buddy! Friendship and Learning Across the Grades*. Oakland, Calif.: Developmental Studies Center.

Christensen, L. (Autumn 1994). "Building Community from Chaos." *Rethinking Schools*: 1, 14–17.

Clayton, L. O. (1985). "The Impact Upon Child-Rearing Attitudes, of Parental Views of the Nature of Humankind." *Journal of Psychology and Christianity* 4, 3: 49–55.

Cline, F., and J. Fay. (1990). *Parenting with Love and Logic: Teaching Children Responsibility*. Colorado Springs, Colo.: Piñon Press.

Collis, M., and J. Dalton. (1990). *Becoming Responsible Learners: Strategies for Positive Classroom Management*. Portsmouth, N.H.: Heinemann.

Crockenberg, V. (Autumn 1982). "Assertive Discipline: A Dissent." *California Journal of Teacher Education* 9: 59–74.

Curwin, R. L., and A.N. Mendler. (1988). *Discipline with Dignity*. Alexandria, Va.: ASCD.

Curwin, R. L., and A.N. Mendler. (March 1989). "We Repeat, Let the Buyer Beware: A Response to Canter." *Educational Leadership:* 83.

Curwin, R. L., and A. N. Mendler. (1991). *Curwin and Mendler's Discipline with Dignity*. Videotape series. Bloomington, Ind.: National Education Service.

Dabney, J., S. Wilson, R. Cavin, and V. Holloway. (1994). "Having a Great Day at Chickasha." In *Innovative Discipline*. New Haven, Conn.: NEA Teacher-to-Teacher Books.

D'Amico, J. (October 1980). "Reviving Student Participation." *Educational Leadership*: 44–46.

de Charms, R. (1968). *Personal Causation: The Internal Affective Determinants of Behavior*. Hillsdale, N.J.: Lawrence Erlbaum.

de Charms, R. (March 1977). "Pawn or Origin? Enhancing Motivation in Disaffected Youth." *Educational Leadership*: 444–448.

Deci, E. L., J. Nezlek, and L. Sheinman. (1981). "Characteristics of the Rewarder and Intrinsic Motivation of the Rewardee." *Journal of Personality and Social Psychology* 40: 1–10.

Deci, E. L., and R. M. Ryan. (1985). *Intrinsic Motivation and Self-Determination in Human Behavior*. New York: Plenum.

Deci, E. L., and R. M. Ryan. (1990). "A Motivational Approach to Self: Integration in Personality." In *Nebraska Symposium on Motivation,* vol. 38, edited by R. Dienstbier. Lincoln: University of Nebraska Press.

Deci, E. L., N. H. Spiegel, R. M. Ryan, R. Koestner, and M. Kauffman. (1982). "Effects of Performance Standards on Teaching Styles: Behavior of Controlling Teachers." *Journal of Educational Psychology* 74: 852–859.

DeVries, R., and B. Zan. (1994). *Moral Classrooms, Moral Children: Creating a Constructivist Atmosphere in Early Education*. New York: Teachers College Press.

Dinkmeyer, D., and G. D. McKay. (1989). *The Parent's Handbook,* 3rd ed. Circle Pines, Minn.: American Guidance Service.

Dore, A. (18 March 1994). "Miracle Cure or Cruel Trick?" *Times Educational Supplement:* sec. 2, pp. 1–2.

Dreikurs, R. (1968). *Psychology in the Classroom*. 2nd ed. New York: Harper & Row.

Dreikurs, R., and P. Cassel. (1972). *Discipline Without Tears*. Reprinted 1991. New York: Plume.

Dreikurs, R., and L. Grey. (1968). *Logical Consequences: A New Approach to Discipline*. Reprinted 1993. New York: Plume.

Dreikurs, R., B. B. Grunwald, and F. C. Pepper. (1982). *Maintaining Sanity in the Classroom: Classroom Management Techniques*. 2nd ed. New York: HarperCollins.

Edwards, C. P. (1986). *Promoting Social and Moral Development in Young Children: Creative Approaches for the Classroom*. New York: Teachers College Press.

Emmer, E. T., and A. Aussiker. (1990). "School and Classroom Discipline Programs: How Well Do They Work?" In *Student Discipline Strategies: Research and Practice*, edited by O. C. Moles. Albany: State University of New York Press.

Emmer, E. T., and C. M. Evertson. (January 1981). "Synthesis of Research on Classroom Management." *Eduational Leadership:* 342–347.

Faber, A., and E. Mazlish. (1995). *How to Talk So Kids Can Learn*. New York: Rawson.

Fabes, R. A., J. Fultz, N. Eisenberg, T. May-Plumlee, and F. S. Christopher. (1989). "Effects of Rewards on Children's Prosocial Motivation: A Socialization Study." *Developmental Psychology* 25: 509–515.

Feshbach, N. D., S. Feshbach, M. Fauvre, and M. Ballard-Campbell. (1983). *Learning to Care: Classroom Activities for Social and Affective Development*. Glenview, Ill.: Scott, Foresman.

Foot, H. C., M. J. Morgan, and R. H. Shute, eds. (1990). *Children Helping Children*. Chichester, England: John Wiley & Sons.

Glasser, W. (1969). *Schools Without Failure*. New York: Harper and Row.

Glasser, W. (1986). *Control Theory in the Classroom*. New York: Harper and Row.

Goodman, J. (1992). *Elementary Schooling for Critical Democracy*. Albany: State University of New York Press.

Gordon, T. (1974). *T.E.T. Teacher Effectiveness Training*. New York: David McKay Co.

Gordon, T. (1989). *Teaching Children Self-Discipline . . . at Home and at School*. New York: Times Books. Reprinted 1991 as *Discipline that Works: Promoting Self-Discipline in Children at Home and at School*. New York: NAL.

Gossen, D. C. (1992). *Restitution: Restructuring School Discipline*. Chapel Hill, N.C.: New View Publications.

Grusec, J. E. (1991). "Socializing Concern for Others in the Home." *Developmental Psychology* 27: 338–342.

Hill, D. (April 1990). "Order in the Classroom." *Teacher Magazine:* 70–77.

Hoffman, M. L., and H. D. Saltzstein. (1967). "Parent Discipline and the Child's Moral Development." *Journal of Personality and Social Psychology* 5: 45–57.

Hyman, I. A. (1990). *Reading, Writing, and the Hickory Stick: The Appalling Story of Physical and Psychological Abuse in American Schools*. Lexington, Mass.: Lexington Books.

Jones, F. H. (June 1979). "The Gentle Art of Classroom Discipline." *The National Elementary Principal:* 26–32.

Kamii, C. (May 1984). "Obedience Is Not Enough." *Young Children:* 11–14.

Kamii, C. (1991). "Toward Autonomy: The Importance of Critical Thinking and Choice Making." *School Psychology Review* 20: 382–388.

Kamii, C., F. B. Clark, and A. Dominick. (May 1994). "The Six National Goals: A Road to Disappointment." *Phi Delta Kappan:* 672–677.

Katz, L. G. (July 1984). "The Professional Early Childhood Teacher." *Young Children:* 3–9.

Katz, L. G. (January 1985). "Katz Responds to Daniels." *Young Children:* 2–3.

Kilpatrick, W. (1992). *Why Johnny Can't Tell Right from Wrong*. New York: Simon & Schuster.

Koestner, R., R. M. Ryan, F. Bernieri, and K. Holt. (1984). "Setting Limits on Children's Behavior: The Differential Effects of Controlling vs. Informational Styles on Intrinsic Motivation and Creativity." *Journal of Personality* 52: 233–248.

Kohlberg, L., and R. Mayer. (1972). "Development as the Aim of Education." *Harvard Educational Review* 42: 449–496.

Kohn, A. (1990a). *The Brighter Side of Human Nature: Altruism and Empathy in Everyday Life.* New York: Basic.

Kohn, A. (1990b). *You Know What They Say . . . : The Truth About Popular Beliefs.* New York: HarperCollins.

Kohn, A. (January 1990c). "The ABCs of Caring." *Teacher Magazine:* 52–58.

Kohn, A. (February 1991). "Group Grade Grubbing Versus Cooperative Learning." *Educational Leadership:* 83–87.

Kohn, A. (1992). *No Contest: The Case Against Competition.* Rev. ed. Boston: Houghton Mifflin.

Kohn, A. (1993a). *Punished by Rewards: The Trouble with Gold Stars, Incentive Plans, A's, Praise, and Other Bribes.* Boston: Houghton Mifflin.

Kohn, A. (September 1993b). "Choices for Children: Why and How to Let Students Decide." *Phi Delta Kappan:* 8–20.

Kohn, A. (October 1994). "Grading: The Issue Is Not How but Why." *Educational Leadership:* 38–41.

Kounin, J. S. (1970). *Discipline and Group Management in Classrooms.* New York: Holt, Rinehart and Winston.

LeCompte, M. (1978). "Learning to Work: The Hidden Curriculum of the Classroom." *Anthropology and Education Quarterly* 9: 22–37.

Lewin, T. (7 December 1995). "Parents Poll Shows Child Abuse to Be More Common." *New York Times:* B16.

Lewis, C. C. (1995). *Educating Hearts and Minds: Reflections on Japanese Preschool and Elementary Education.* Cambridge, England: Cambridge University Press.

Lewis, C. C., E. Schaps, and M. Watson. (March 1995). "Beyond the Pendulum: Creating Challenging and Caring Schools." *Phi Delta Kappan:* 547–554.

Lickona, T., and M. Paradise. (1980). "Democracy in the Elementary School." In *Moral Education: A First Generation of Research and Development,* edited by R. Mosher. New York: Praeger.

Lovett, H. (1985). *Cognitive Counseling and Persons with Special Needs.* New York: Praeger.

McBride, M. E. (May 1995). "The Italian Restaurant Project: Lessons of Restructuring." *Educational Leadership:* 64–66.

McCaslin, M., and T. L. Good. (April 1992). "Compliant Cognition: The Misalliance of Management and the Instructional Goals in Current School Reform." *Educational Researcher:* 4–17.

McCord, J. (1991). "Questioning the Value of Punishment." *Social Problems* 38: 167–179.

McDaniel, T. R. (February 1982). "How to Be an Effective Authoritarian: A Back-to-Basics Approach to Classroom Discipline." *The Clearing House:* 245–247.

McLaughlin, M. W. (1993). "What Matters Most in Teachers' Workplace Context?" In *Teachers' Work: Individuals, Colleagues, and Context,* edited by J. W. Little and M. W. McLaughlin. New York: Teachers College Press.

McNeil, L. M. (1986). *Contradictions of Control: School Structure and School Knowledge.* New York: Routledge and Kegan Paul.

Meier, D. (1995). *The Power of Their Ideas: Lessons for America from a Small School in Harlem*. Boston: Beacon.

Midgley, C., H. Feldlaufer, and J. S. Eccles. (1988). "The Transition to Junior High School: Beliefs of Pre- and Posttransition Teachers." *Journal of Youth and Adolescence* 17: 543–562.

Molnar, A., and B. Lindquist. (1989). *Changing Problem Behavior in Schools*. San Francisco: Jossey-Bass.

Morse, W. C. (Summer 1987). "Introduction." *Teaching Exceptional Children:* 4–6.

National Association for the Education of Young Children. (1986). "Helping Children Learn Self-Control: A Guide to Discipline." Pamphlet. Washington, D.C.: NAEYC.

Nelsen, J. (1987). *Positive Discipline*. New York: Ballantine.

Nelsen, J., L. Lott, and H. S. Glenn. (1993). *Positive Discipline in the Classroom*. Rocklin, Calif.: Prima.

Nicholls, J.G., and S. P. Hazzard. (1993). *Education as Adventure: Lessons from the Second Grade*. New York: Teachers College Press.

Paley, V. G. (1992). *You Can't Say You Can't Play*. Cambridge, Mass.: Harvard University Press.

Palma, L. (Fall 1994). "Living in the Gray." *NAIS Academic Forum:* 8–9.

Pavlan, B.N. (October 1992). "The Benefits of Nongraded Schools." *Educational Leadership:* 22–25.

Phelan, T. W. (1995). *1-2-3 Magic: Training Your Children to Do What You Want*. Glen Ellyn, Ill.: Child Management, Inc.

Piaget, J. (1965). *The Moral Judgment of the Child*. New York: Free Press.

Power, F. C., A. Higgins, and L. Kohlberg. (1989). *Lawrence Kohlberg's Approach to Moral Education*. New York: Columbia University Press.

Render, G. F., J. M. Padilla, and H. M. Krank. (1989). "Assertive Discipline: A Critical Review and Analysis." *Teachers College Record* 90: 607–630.

Ryan, K. (1989). "In Defense of Character Education." In *Moral Development and Character Education: A Dialogue*, edited by L. P. Nucci. Berkeley, Calif.: McCutchan.

Ryan, R. M., R. Koestner, and E. L. Deci. (1991). "Ego-Involved Persistence: When Free-Choice Behavior Is Not Intrinsically Motivated." *Motivation and Emotion* 15: 185–205.

Sapon-Shevin, M. (1994). *Playing Favorites: Gifted Education and the Disruption of Community*. Albany: State University of New York Press.

Schaps, E. (June 1990). "Cooperative Learning: The Challenge in the '90s." *Cooperative Learning Magazine:* 5–8.

Scott-Little, M. C., and S. D. Holloway. (1992). "Child Care Providers' Reasoning About Misbehaviors." *Early Childhood Research Quarterly* 7: 595–606.

Sergiovanni, T. J. (1994). *Building Community in Schools*. San Francisco: Jossey-Bass.

Shanker, A. (6 December 1995). "Why Schools Need Standards and Innovation." *Education Week:* 48, 37.

Slavin, R. E. (1995). *Cooperative Learning*. 2nd ed. Boston: Allyn and Bacon.

Solomon, D., M. Watson, V. Battistich, E. Schaps, and K. Delucchi. (1992). "Creating a Caring Community: Educational Practices That Promote Children's Prosocial Development." In *Effective and Responsible Teaching,* ed. by F. K. Oser, A. Dick, and J. Patry. San Francisco: Jossey-Bass.

Straus, M. A. (1994). *Beating the Devil Out of Them: Corporal Punishment in American Families.* Lexington, Mass.: Lexington Books.

Toby, J. (Winter 1993/94). "Everyday School Violence: How Disorder Fuels It." *American Educator:* 4–9, 44–48.

Watson, M. S. (Autumn 1984). "Knowing What Children Are Really Like: Implications for Teacher Education." *Teacher Education Quarterly* 11, 4: 35–49.

Watson, M., D. Solomon, V. Battistich, E. Schaps, and J. Solomon. (1989). "The Child Development Project: Combining Traditional and Developmental Approaches to Values Education." In *Moral Development and Character Education: A Dialogue,* edited by L. P. Nucci. Berkeley, Calif.: McCutchan.

Wilson, I. (13 January 1995). "Prepare to Take Effective Control." *Times Educational Supplement:* A6.

Wynne, E. (1989). "Transmitting Traditional Values in Contemporary Schools." In *Moral Development and Character Education: A Dialogue,* edited by L. P. Nucci. Berkeley, Calif.: McCutchan.

Zahn-Waxler, C., M. Radke-Yarrow, E. Wagner, and M. Chapman. (1992). "Development of Concern for Others." *Developmental Psychology* 28: 126–136.

∞

# INDEX

coercion, 22–24
Coloroso, Barbara, 143
community, school as
academic learning as related to,
103, 117–118
and choices for students, 118–
119
definition of, 101–102
effects of student expulsion on,
140
prerequisites for creating, 109–
110
reasons for creating, 103–105
and relationships among adults,
110
vs. focus on discipline, control,
and rules, xiv, 63, 71, 73, 105,
107
vs. pseudocommunity, 108–109
vs. school as collective, 107–
108, 152n2
vs. use of peer pressure to
elicit conformity, 108
ways of creating, 110–119
ways of destroying, 106–107
competition, 105–106, 117
compliance by students, efforts to
elicit
as analogous to right answers
in academics, 65–66
euphemisms for:
"motivation," 144
"responsibility," 145
"self-discipline," 83
as goal of New Disciplines,
58–60
as goal of traditional discipline,
56–58
as inimical to moral development, 62–68, 77, 84–85, 119
predictors of success at, 63, 81
used by some teachers more
than others, 62–63
vs. improving the curriculum,
18–21, 125
vs. meeting students' needs,
9–10

vs. reconsidering one's demands, 12–16, 124–125
conflict
resolution of, by students in
communities, 103
resolution vs. elimination of, 74
value of, 74–77
consequences. See Logical consequences; Natural consequences;
Punishment
constructivism, 66–67, 78
as alternative to eliciting students' compliance, 67–68
implications of:
for role of conflict, 74–77
for use of rules, 71–74
as relevant to social and moral
development, xv, 67–68, 92
vs. internalization, 83
control of classroom, teacher's
chaos counterposed to, 2, 63, 142
class meeting used to achieve,
89, 91–92
curriculum used to achieve, 64n
disguised with pseudochoices,
48–52
effects of, on students' decision
making, 78, 84
as goal of:
Assertive Discipline, 55
classroom management,
56–58
New Disciplines, 58–60
negative effects of, 7, 18, 58,
62, 142
rationalized as temporarily necessary, 64–65
reasons for seeking, 64, 100
vs. teacher's relationships with
students, 112
Cooperative Discipline
blaming students in, 17–18,
147n3
compliance as goal of, 59
and curriculum, 20
intolerance of, for students'
objections, 75

"logical consequences" (*cont'd*)
  in books for parents, 143
  examples of, 41–44
  as punitive, 24, 39–45
lunchroom, problems in, 126
lying, 16

*Magic 1-2-3*, 56
Mansbridge, Jane, 151*n*7
Mazlish, Elaine, 47, 50, 143
McNeil, Linda, 64*n*
Meier, Deborah, 109, 150*n*3, 151*n*7
Mendler, Allen. *See* Discipline with
  Dignity
Milgram, Stanley, 84–85
misbehavior. *See* Discipline problems
moral development, promoting
  by fostering relationships
    among students, 103
  by giving students opportuni-
    ties to choose, 78, 83–85
  by helping students construct
    moral meaning, 67–68, 142
  through use of literature, 117–
    118
  in younger vs. older students,
    150*n*3
  vs. creating community devoid
    of student choice, 119
  vs. eliciting compliance, 65–67
  vs. focusing on internalization
    of values, 83
  vs. imposing specific rules,
    72–73
  vs. reinforcing behaviors, 69–70
  vs. using punitive conse-
    quences, 28–29
multi-age classrooms, 104

National Association for the Education of Young Children, 47–48,
  150*n*3
National Association of Independent Schools, 15
"natural consequences," 51–52
needs of children, 9–10, 23*n*, 81

Nelsen, Jane, 38, 39, 41, 42, 44, 52–
  53, 71, 87, 128, 146*n*2
"New Disciplines," xiii, 37–38, 45,
  49, 52–53, 58–60, 68, 138. *See
  also* Cooperative Discipline; Discipline with Dignity; etc.
Nicholls, John, 57–58, 63
Noddings, Nel, 10

Paley, Vivian, 47
parents
  problems reported to, 24, 40,
    132–133
  resources for, 56, 143
  use of traditional discipline by,
    143
peer pressure, eliciting conformity
  through, 35–36, 44, 108, 149*n*8
perspective taking, 89, 113–114
Piaget, Jean, 54, 67, 103
Positive Discipline, 52–53, 150*n*11.
  *See also* Nelsen, Jane
positive reinforcement. *See* Praise;
  Rewards
power, as lesson of coercion and
  punishment, 24, 27, 140
praise
  assumptions about human
    nature underlying use of, 3
  collective, 35–36
  problems with, 35–36, 69–70, 139
  public, 35, 72
  vs. authentic dialogue, 112
principal, sending students to, as
  punishment, 25
prison, 139–140
problem solving
  activities to help teachers get
    better at, 129–136
  authentic vs. perfunctory
    attempts at, 126–127
  and diagnosis of problem's
    cause, 123–124
  examples of, 78–79, 82, 89–90,
    93–94, 96, 115, 129–132
  instructional design as related
    to, 128*n*

# ABOUT THE AUTHOR

Alfie Kohn, a former teacher turned author and lecturer, writes and speaks widely on human behavior, education, and social theory. His four previous books are: *No Contest: The Case Against Competition* (Houghton Mifflin, 1986; rev. ed. 1992), *The Brighter Side of Human Nature: Altruism and Empathy in Everyday Life* (Basic Books, 1990), *You Know What They Say . . . : The Truth About Popular Beliefs* (HarperCollins, 1990), and *Punished by Rewards: The Trouble with Gold Stars, Incentive Plans, A's, Praise, and Other Bribes* (Houghton Mifflin, 1993).

Kohn's criticisms of competition and rewards have helped to shape the thinking of educators—as well as parents and managers—across the country and abroad. He has appeared on more than 200 TV and radio programs, including "Oprah" and the "Today" show; his work has been described on the front page of the *Wall Street Journal,* in *U.S. News and World Report,* the *Harvard Education Letter,* and dozens of other magazines and newspapers. His own articles, meanwhile, have appeared in most of the major education periodicals, including *Educational Leadership, Phi Delta Kappan,* and *Education Week,* as well as in such publications as the *Atlantic Monthly,* the *Nation,* the *Harvard Business Review, Parenting,* and the *New York Times.*

Kohn speaks frequently at national conferences and conducts workshops for teachers, administrators, parents, and researchers. Educated at Brown University and the University of Chicago, he lives with his wife and daughter in the Boston area. He can be reached at 242 School St., Belmont, MA 02178.